Lotus 1-2-3™
Models

Lotus 1-2-3™
Models

by
Gilbert Held

Weber Systems, Inc.
Cleveland, Ohio

The authors have exercised due care in the preparation of this book and the programs contained in it. The authors and the publisher make no warranties either express or implied with regard to the information and programs contained in this book. In no event shall the authors or publisher be liable for incidental or consequential damages arising out of the furnishing, performance, or any information and/or programs.

Published by:
Weber Systems, Inc.
8437 Mayfield Road
Cleveland, Ohio 44026

For information or translations and book distributors outside of the United States, please contact WSI at the above address.

Lotus 1-2-3™ Models

Library of Congress Cataloging in Publication
Main entry under title:

Lotus 1-2-3 models

   Includes index
   1. Lotus 1-2-3 (Computer program) 2. Business—Data processing I. Title.
HF5548.4.L67H45 1985   001.64'25   85-701
ISBN 0-938862-29-4

Typesetting and Layout: Tina Koran and Susan Zaksheske

Contents

Preface

Similar to the manner in which the industrial revolution changed society in the early 1900's, the growth of personal computer utilization has provided individuals with a mechanism to restructure the way they work. Until recently, the emphasis of most software developers was focused upon business programs and entertainment packages. Even though many programs are reaching the marketplace that address the requirements of the home user and civic organizations, the aggregate cost of such programs is normally prohibitive. At the other end of the spectrum, most businesses can satisfy a majority of their personal computer software requirements by the purchase of a few programs that include an electronic spreadsheet, a word processor and perhaps several accounting programs.

Since an electronic spreadsheet program is by far the most popularly used personal computer software, the ability to use the power and capability of this program for home and civic organization functions would be most desirable and has resulted in the focus of this book. In fact, the credit for this book, in part, can be attributed to my son Jonathan. In attempting to explain the use of an electronic spreadsheet program to a person in grade school, I found that economic models and forecasting were of far less interest than the ability of the program to maintain a membership list, telephone directory and similar functions.

Thus, in addition to developing several financial models that provide the reader with the capability to forecast the effect of retirement funding, one's tax status and other financial related topics, we have focused our attention on developing models to perform applications that would normally require the purchase of separate programs. Models included in this category will be developed to generate mailing lists, maintain one's checkbook balance, perform grade recording functions, develop and maintain attendance lists and perform other functions that would normally require one to purchase separate programs. From a cost benefit perspective, implementing just a few of the models presented in this book will make one's electronic spreadsheet program into the most cost effective category of software one can purchase.

The models presented in this book can be developed on most electronic spreadsheet programs. These models should be viewed by the reader in a similar fashion to the process of selecting the fabric of a suit of clothes, since once the model is selected it may require tailoring to meet a specific requirement. By our elaboration upon the concept of each model and discussion of their construction and potential modifications, the reader should be able to easily tailor them to his or her specific requirements.

Although many spreadsheet programs can be used to develop the models presented in this book, we selected 1-2-3 by Lotus Development Corporation to use as our development tool. Since each model is explained and developed as a separate entity using a variety of 1-2-3 commands, this book also can serve as a tutorial or refresher manual in the use of this electronic spreadsheet program. In fact, it is recommended that the reader use the index of this book to locate 1-2-3 commands, functions, or operations that he or she may not be familiar with and then read the relevant portion of this book that explains their usage.

From a personal perspective, I enjoyed writing this book and hope that the material presented herein will provide the reader with many practical applications that can be readily implemented on his or her spreadsheet.

INTRODUCTION

The goal of this book is to provide the reader with a detailed, step-by-step guide to the construction of practical spreadsheet models that can be used in the home or by civic organizations. In constructing the models presented in this book, we used the 1-2-3 spreadsheet program developed by Lotus Development Corporation as a development tool. However, most spreadsheet programs can be used to develop a majority of the models presented in this book.

Since 1-2-3 will be used as our development tool, we will include the relevant 1-2-3 commands required to build each of the models presented in this chapter. Thus, in addition to illustrating how a variety of models can be developed to satisfy the requirements of the home user and civic organizations, this book can also be used as a tutorial guide to the use of 1-2-3 commands.

Since each chapter covers the development of a single model as an entity, the reader can skip one or more chapters that may not be applicable to his or her requirements. In addition, since the commands required to develop each model are explained as they are presented in each chapter, the reader does not have to worry about reading this book in sequence to understand how one or more formulas work.

Formula Presentation

Each 1-2-3 formula presented in this book follows the method of presentation in the Lotus 1-2-3 manual. Thus, letters in bold type indicate the characters the user must enter to generate the appropriate 1-2-3 function. The symbol ↵ included at the end of some commands indicates

11

that the enter or return key must be pressed to initiate the command. The absence of this symbol after other commands indicates that those commands are immediately executed after the last character is entered.

File Operations

In this book, we have assumed that the reader has entered his or her disk operating system in drive A. After the disk operating system is initialized and 1-2-3 is brought up by entering the command **123**, we have assumed that a formatted diskette has been placed in drive B. Thus, in this book we will save our models onto this diskette by issuing the 1-2-3 command:

/File,Save,**B:FILENAME**⏎

to save each model on the diskette in drive B.

1-2-3 is a powerful and flexible tool that is limited only by the imagination of the people who use it. It is hoped that the models presented in this book will expand upon the reader's imagination as well as provide the reader with a step by step guide to developing models to satify his or her requirements.

To facilitate the utilization of spreadsheet programs produced by other vendors, we have included the following table that compares the features of SuperCalc[3] as well as four other spreadsheet models to 1-2-3. Readers can use the entries in this table to quickly compare the capability of each spreadsheet to 1-2-3. Doing so will permit the reader to determine if he or she can easily construct one of the models presented in this book by using another spreadsheet or if one will have to consider extensive modification to the model to obtain the equivalent 1-2-3 function.

SPREADSHEET FUNCTION COMPARISON

Feature	Lotus 1-2-3	SuperCalc²	SuperCalc³	VisiCalc IV	Multiplan	Context MBA
Minimum Memory Requirements	128	64	96	128	64	256
Spreadsheet:						
Rows	2048	254	254	254	255	999
Columns	256	63	63	63	63	95
Variable Column Width	Yes	Yes	Yes	Yes	Yes	Yes
Field Alignment:						
Left	Yes	Yes	Yes	Yes	Yes	Yes
Right	Yes	Yes	Yes	Yes	Yes	Yes
Center	Yes	Yes	Yes	Yes	Yes	Yes
Display:						
Integer	Yes	Yes	Yes	Yes	Yes	Yes
Exponential	Yes	Yes	Yes	Yes	Yes	Yes
Percentage	Yes	Yes	Yes	Yes	Yes	Yes
Dollar Sign	Yes	Yes	Yes	Yes	Yes	Yes
Cell Protection	Yes	Yes	Yes	Yes	Yes	Yes
Math Functions:						
Average	Yes	Yes	Yes	Yes	Yes	Yes
Sum	Yes	Yes	Yes	Yes	Yes	Yes
Round	Yes	Yes	Yes	Yes	Yes	Yes
Square Root	Yes	Yes	Yes	Yes	Yes	Yes
Log	Yes	Yes	Yes	Yes	Yes	Yes
Sine	Yes	Yes	Yes	Yes	Yes	Yes
Cosine	Yes	Yes	Yes	Yes	Yes	Yes
Tangent	Yes	Yes	Yes	Yes	Yes	Yes
Pi	Yes	Yes	Yes	Yes	Yes	Yes
Financial Functions:						
Net Present Value	Yes	Yes	Yes	Yes	Yes	Yes
Future Value	Yes	No	Yes	Yes	No	No
Internal Rate of Return	No	No	Yes	No	No	Yes
Annuity	Yes	No	Yes	No	No	No
Date Arithmetic	Yes	Yes	Yes	Yes	Yes	Yes
Logical Functions:						
If Then Else	Yes	Yes	Yes	Yes	Yes	Yes
And	Yes	Yes	Yes	Yes	Yes	Yes
Or	Yes	Yes	Yes	Yes	Yes	Yes

table continued on next page

Feature	Lotus 1-2-3	SuperCalc²	SuperCalc³	VisiCalc IV	Multiplan	Context MBA
Not	Yes	Yes	Yes	Yes	Yes	Yes
Error	Yes	Yes	Yes	Yes	Yes	Yes
Table Lookup	Yes	Yes	Yes	Yes	Yes	Yes
Data Management:						
Sort	Yes	Yes	Yes	Yes	Yes	Yes
Partial Row/Column	Yes	Yes	Yes	No	Yes	Yes
Graphics Charts:						
Bar	Yes	No	Yes	Yes	No	Yes
Line	Yes	No	Yes	Yes	No	Yes
Pie	Yes	No	Yes	Yes	No	Yes
Hi-Lo-Close	No	No	Yes	Yes	No	Yes
Scatter	Yes	No	Yes	Yes	No	Yes
Print Formatting:						
Headers	Yes	No	No	Yes	No	Yes
Footers	Yes	No	No	No	No	Yes
Page Numbering	Yes	Yes	Yes	Yes	Yes	Yes
Sideways Printing	No	No	No	Yes	No	No
Printer Setup String	Yes	Yes	Yes	Yes	Yes	Yes
Plotter Support	Yes	No	Yes	No	No	No
Graphics Printer Support	Yes	No	Yes	Yes	No	Yes

1

The Attendance List

Concept

An attendance list or roster is commonly used by many types of organizations as well as for classroom activities. Normally, this type of list contains the names of the persons registered for a specific activity in the first column and has one or more columns of events that are checked to represent the presence or absence of a person at a particular period in time.

Developing the Model

Since we will have a list of names in the first column, we will assign a heading to this column. In our example, we will label column A with the heading "TROOP #23", however, we could obviously use such labels as

"GEOGRAPHY," "STATISTICS," or simply "MEMBER" to reflect the specific type of attendance list we wish to develop. Since the default column width of 1-2-3 is 9 character positions, we may wish to increase the width of the first column if our attendance list contains members with long last names or we wish to include both the first and last name or each person in one column.

Let us assume that we wish to increase the width of column A to 20 postions. This amount should normally be sufficient to contain a last name followed by a comma and then a first name. We can increase the width of column A to 20 positions by positioning the active cell to any cell in column A and issuing the /**WCS** command to change the format as follows:

/**W**orksheet,**C**olumn-Width,**S**et,**20**⏎

With the width of column A set to 20 positions, let us enter our heading followed by five member names which we will place in rows 3 through 7 of column A. Our initial model might appear as follows:

```
A1:  'TROOP #23                                              READY


               A              B       C       D       E       F
 1    TROOP #23
 2
 3    Kavinolski, Ronald
 4    Duck, Donald
 5    Mouse, Mickey
 6    Smith, John
 7    Duck, Daffy
 8
 9
10
11
12
13
14
15
16
17
18
19
20
```

Suppose we anticipate Troop #23 will have 8 meetings during the year. We could label 8 columns with either a meeting number or date horizontally across row 1. Since most attendance lists only require an appropriate space to check-off the fact that a member attended a meeting, we may simply wish to enter a pair of brackets throughout each column that corresponds to a Troop #23 meeting. With the default width of each column being 9 positions, we could either include several meetings in each column or reduce the column width to correspond to the size of our headings. Note that the headings will be followed by bracket pairs that will be entered down each column to correspond to member names for check-off at each meeting.

Suppose we wish to include the month and day as our column heading. Then, the maximum number of character positions required to denote each meeting would be 5 since we could enter mm/dd as the heading, with mm denoting the month and dd the day of the month for the meeting. For certain meetings, as few as 3 positions would be required since a meeting on January 3 could be labeled as 1/3.

Let us assume we wish to allocate 5 character positions in each column for the meeting date heading which will permit us to print the entire attendance list as one entity. We can set the width of all columns in the spreadsheet that are not already explicitly set to 5 character positions with the /**WGC** command by entering:

/**W**orksheet,**G**lobal,**C**olumn-Width,**5**↵

Our display would now appear as follows:

```
A1: 'TROOP #23                                                    READY


              A         B    C    D    E    F    G    H    I    J    K
 1   TROOP #23
 2
 3   Kavinolski, Ronald
 4   Duck, Donald
 5   Mouse, Mickey
 6   Smith, John
 7   Duck, Daffy
 8
 9
10
11
12
13
14
15
16
17
18
19
20
```

If we start to enter meeting dates across row 1, once we begin to use 5 digits for a date we will notice that there is no space between the date entered into each cell.

Suppose the first date that requires 5 digits for representation is the eighth entry. For clarity, we would most likely want to change the width of column I to 6 positions. This can be accomplished by moving the active cell to any cell in column I and then using the /**WCS** command again as follows:

/**W**orksheet,**C**olumn-Width,**S**et,6⤶

Prior to actually entering the meeting dates across row 1, we should remember that we want these dates to be treated as text. To accomplish this, we must precede each date by a single quotation (') mark. Otherwise, as an example, entering 1/23 into cell B1 would result in the value of 1 divided by 23 being entered into that cell.

Let us assume the 8 meeting dates for Troop #23 are as indicated in the following table:

TROOP #23 MEETINGS

1/23	5/12
3/15	6/11
3/28	9/18
4/15	10/14

We can enter each meeting date in cell B1 through I1 by prefixing the date with single quotation marks so they will be treated as text. After the 8 dates have been entered, our screen should appear as follows:

```
I2:                                                                    READY

                    A        B     C     D     E     F     G     H      I
1   TROOP #23               1/23  3/15  3/28  4/15  5/12  6/11  9/18  10/14
2
3   Kavinolski, Ronald
4   Duck, Donald
5   Mouse, Mickey
6   Smith, John
7   Duck, Daffy
8
9
10
11
12
13
14
15
16
17
18
19
20
```

Since we wish to simply have a mechanism to check attendance, a pair of brackets separated by a space may be sufficient for our requirements. We can first enter a pair of brackets separated by a space into cell B3 and then copy the bracket throughout the cells that represent meetings which each member of Troop #23 might attend. Once the bracket pair is entered into cell B3, we can use the /C command as follows:

/Copy,B3-⌐,B4.B7-⌐

The preceding command would copy the entry in cell B3 into cells B4 through B7. To copy the bracket pair across each row, we would again use the /C command. Thus,

/Copy,B3-⌐,C3.I3-⌐

would copy the bracket pair through cells C3 through I3. Similarly, we would copy the bracket pair across each row until our screen would appear as follows:

```
B3:  '[ ]                                                                    READY

              A            B      C      D      E      F      G      H      I
1    TROOP #23           1/23   3/15   3/28   4/15   5/12   6/11   9/18   10/14
2
3    Kavinolski, Ronald  [ ]    [ ]    [ ]    [ ]    [ ]    [ ]    [ ]    [ ]
4    Duck, Donald        [ ]    [ ]    [ ]    [ ]    [ ]    [ ]    [ ]    [ ]
5    Mouse, Mickey       [ ]    [ ]    [ ]    [ ]    [ ]    [ ]    [ ]    [ ]
6    Smith, John         [ ]    [ ]    [ ]    [ ]    [ ]    [ ]    [ ]    [ ]
7    Duck, Daffy         [ ]    [ ]    [ ]    [ ]    [ ]    [ ]    [ ]    [ ]
8
9
10
11
12
13
14
15
16
17
18
19
20
```

We could also use one /C command instead of many once the bracket pairs are entered into column B. Here the command

/Copy,B3⏎,C3.I7⏎

would also fill our screen from cells B3 through I7 with bracket pairs.

ORDERING THE LIST

Although we randomly entered five names into column A, suppose we have many members in our troop. In such circumstances, it might be easier to work with a sorted attendance list. To arrange the names in the list in sorted order we can use the /DSDP command as follows:

/Data,Sort,Data-Range,A3.A7⏎,Primary-Key,A3⏎,A⏎,Go

The result of this command will cause rows 3 through 7 in column A to be sorted in ascending order. Our display would now appear as follows:

```
A3:  'Duck, Daffy                                                    READY

                   A         B      C      D      E      F      G      H      I
 1    TROOP #23           1/23   3/15   3/28   4/15   5/12   6/11   9/18  10/14
 2
 3    Duck, Daffy        [ ]    [ ]    [ ]    [ ]    [ ]    [ ]    [ ]    [ ]
 4    Duck, Donald       [ ]    [ ]    [ ]    [ ]    [ ]    [ ]    [ ]    [ ]
 5    Kavinolski, Ronald [ ]    [ ]    [ ]    [ ]    [ ]    [ ]    [ ]    [ ]
 6    Mouse, Mickey      [ ]    [ ]    [ ]    [ ]    [ ]    [ ]    [ ]    [ ]
 7    Smith, John        [ ]    [ ]    [ ]    [ ]    [ ]    [ ]    [ ]    [ ]
 8
 9
10
11
12
13
14
15
16
17
18
19
20
```

After we have entered the members of our troop and placed those members in sorted order, the next task we may wish to perform is to obtain a hard copy of our attendance list.

PRINTING THE LIST

Since the boundary of our model is between cells A1 and I7, we can use the following /**PPR** command to print our attendance list.

/**P**rint,**P**rinter,**R**ange,**A1.I7**⤶,**G**o,**P**age,**Q**uit

In this command the **R**ange,**A1.I7** directs 1-2-3 to print only the area of the spreadsheet where our model is located, the **G**o, tells 1-2-3 to begin printing, the **P**age forces the printer to the top of a new page, and the **Q**uit tells 1-2-3 that we are through printing. Our output would appear as follows:

```
TROOP #23              1/23   3/15   3/28   4/15   5/12   6/11   9/18  10/14

Duck, Daffy           [ ]    [ ]    [ ]    [ ]    [ ]    [ ]    [ ]    [ ]
Duck, Donald          [ ]    [ ]    [ ]    [ ]    [ ]    [ ]    [ ]    [ ]
Kavinolski, Ronald    [ ]    [ ]    [ ]    [ ]    [ ]    [ ]    [ ]    [ ]
Mouse, Mickey         [ ]    [ ]    [ ]    [ ]    [ ]    [ ]    [ ]    [ ]
Smith, John           [ ]    [ ]    [ ]    [ ]    [ ]    [ ]    [ ]    [ ]
```

Modifications to Consider

For simplicity of illustration, we developed our attendance list based upon having five members in our troop. Since 1-2-3 contains a total of 2048 rows we could expand our attendance list to contain up to 2048 persons which should be more than sufficient for most requirements. If we had more than 2048 members or believed that our membership could expand beyond that number, we could construct two separate models. Thus one model might contain members whose last names started with the letters A through M while the second model would contain members whose surname began with the letters N through Z.

Since nothing is static in life, it might be a good idea to save the model as a file by using the **/FS** (File,Save) command followed by a filename appropriate to represent the attendance list. Then, if new members join the troop or members quit, we could retrieve the model with the **/FR** (Retrieve) command and make the appropriate changes to the list by using the **/WIR** (Worksheet,Insert,Row) command to insert an empty row for new members or the **/WDR** (Worksheet,Delete,Row) command to delete a member from the list.

2

Auction Bid Sheet

Concept

One of the most popularly employed fund raising techniques of civic organizations is the auction. Usually, members of an organization are asked to solicit various merchants in the community to donate articles that are auctioned during some social function. Since donated merchandise is obtained on a random basis, with the amount and quantity of items dependent upon the persuasion skills of the solicitor, it is often just before the actual auction that one knows exactly what items will be available for sale. This is obviously a problem for organizations that wish to give each member a concise, printed bid sheet and represents a function that can be automated by the use of a spreadsheet.

The bid sheet used in some charitable auctions consists of a heading identifying the organization. This is usually followed by two to four columns of tabular data that can contain the item number, a description of the merchandise offered, its estimated retail value and perhaps a minimum or opening bid. The item number is usually a series of sequential numbers starting at unity which denotes the item currently being bid and is used by the auctioneer and auction attendees as a reference point during the auction. The description will vary based upon the merchandise offered and may include the name or affiliation of the merchant who donated the item. If not, one may consider using a separate column in the model to identify the donator.

The decision concerning the addition of an estimated value and minimum bid column is usually governed by members of the auction committee. Although some persons may consider a minimum bid as unnecessary, it does represent a starting point for the auction of each item.

The Bid Sheet Model

For the present our charity will remain anonymous, although we will leave room in our model to add an appropriate heading in row 1. Assuming we wish to include four columns of data for our bid sheet headings, we should determine the width of each column required to contain the necessary information. Let us assume the following column assignments and column widths will satisfy our organization's requirements.

Table 2.1. Column Assignments

Column	Heading	Width
A	ITEM #	9
B	DESCRIPTION	20
C	ESTIMATED VALUE	9
D	MINIMUM BID	9

Since the default column width of 1-2-3 is 9 positions, we must move the active cell to any cell in column B and change column B's width using the /**WCS** command as follows:

/**W**orksheet,**C**olumn-Width,**S**et,**20**↵

Let us enter the column headings into our spreadsheet, using cells C3 and C4 to contain ESTIMATED VALUE and cells D3 and D4 to hold MINIMUM BID so that our model appears as follows:

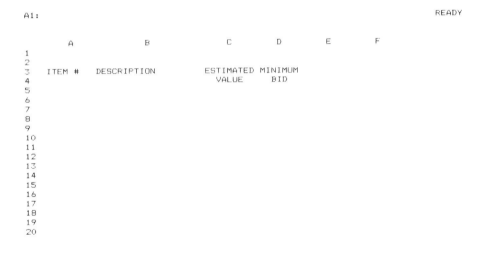

Since there are 9 characters in ESTIMATED, we should enter the heading MINIMUM as text data with a leading single quotation (') mark and a space between the quotation mark and the letter M. This will insure that the heading in cell D3 is separated by one character position from the end of the heading in cell C3. Similarly, we should enter the heading VALUE in cell C3 as ' VALUE to insure it is centered under the heading ESTIMATED.

If we want to underline our headings we can enter the backslash character (\) which is the 1-2-3 symbol for repeating text entry followed by a dash (-) into cell A5. To continue this line of dashes to the end of column D we would use the following /**C** command:

/**C**opy,**A5**↵,**B5.D5**↵

This would result in our model appearing as follows:

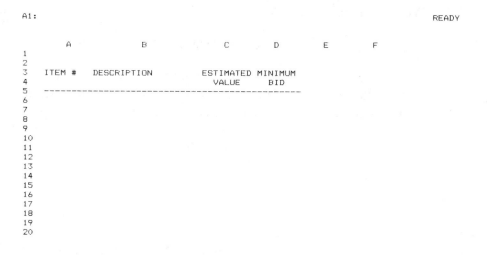

```
A1:                                                                    READY

          A              B              C         D        E        F
 1
 2
 3   ITEM #    DESCRIPTION          ESTIMATED MINIMUM
 4                                    VALUE     BID
 5   ---------------------------------------------------------
 6
 7
 8
 9
10
11
12
13
14
15
16
17
18
19
20
```

Now, let us enter 10 items into our model and see how we can use 1-2-3 to easily update and manipulate the data in our auction bid sheet as additional items are donated.

To automate the generation of items numbers, we can enter 1 into cell A6 and the formula +A6+1 into cell A7. Now we can copy this formula to cells A8 through A15 to automatically generate item numbers through 10. Here, we would enter the command:

/Copy,A7,⅃,A8.A15⅃

Assuming we entered the command:

/Worksheet,Global,Format,Text

to turn the formula display on, our model would appear as follows:

```
A1:                                                                    READY

        A              B              C          D        E        F
1
2
3    ITEM #      DESCRIPTION       ESTIMATED  MINIMUM
4                                    VALUE      BID
5    -----------------------------------------------------------
6               1
7    +A6+1
8    +A7+1
9    +A8+1
10   +A9+1
11   +A10+1
12   +A11+1
13   +A12+1
14   +A13+1
15   +A14+1
16
17
18
19
20
```

If we enter the /**W**orksheet,**G**lobal,**F**ormat,**G**eneral command to turn the formula display off the item numbers will appear right justified in column A.

As a result of entering the preceding /**WGFG** command, our model would appear as follows:

```
A1:                                                                    READY

        A              B              C          D        E        F
1
2
3    ITEM #      DESCRIPTION       ESTIMATED  MINIMUM
4                                    VALUE      BID
5    -----------------------------------------------------------
6               1
7               2
8               3
9               4
10              5
11              6
12              7
13              8
14              9
15             10
16
17
18
19
20
```

Prior to entering 10 items into our bid sheet, let us change columns C and D to display data with two decimal places by entering the following command:

/Range,Format,Fixed,2⏎,C6.D15⏎

In the preceding command, C6.D15 specifies columns C and D rows 6 through 15 as the range while the Fixed,2 informs 1-2-3 that data in these columns are to be displayed in money format with two decimal places.

Now let us assume our organization has received 10 items that were donated for the sale at the auction. After we have entered these items into our model, our spreadsheet will appear similar to figure 2.1.

```
A1:                                                              READY

        A           B              C       D      E       F
 1
 2
 3   ITEM #    DESCRIPTION       ESTIMATED MINIMUM
 4                                VALUE    BID
 5   -------------------------------------------------------------
 6        1 Green Beret           29.95     5.00
 7        2 Word Processor        99.95    10.00
 8        3 Dinner for 2 at Lees  50.00    25.00
 9        4 1 month at Gents SPA  30.00    10.00
10        5 Melex mens watch      74.95    25.00
11        6 Lady's green scarf    15.00     5.00
12        7 Desk lamp             25.00    12.00
13        8 Walnut bookcase       99.95    15.00
14        9 Desk set              15.00     5.00
15       10 IBM PC Game Disk      34.95    15.00
16
17
18
19
20
```

Figure 2.1. Bid Sheet Model

Assuming there are still a few days until the big event, we could save our model onto a disk file with the expectation that we can add additional donations at a later date. Thus, we might enter the command:

/File,Save,B:AUCTION⏎

to save our model on the diskette in drive B with the filename AUCTION.

Modifying the Bid Sheet

Let us assume the solicitors of our organization were very active and obtained five additional donations. To update our auction bid sheet, we would first retrieve the model we previously saved by using the /**FR** command as follows:

/File,Retrieve,**B:AUCTION**⏎

Now, let us add the five additional donations to our model. To obtain item numbers 11 through 15 we can copy the formula in cell A15 into cells A16 through A20, using the /**C** command as follows:

/Copy,**A15,**⏎**,A16.A20**⏎

Upon our entering the preceding /**C** command, the numbers 11 through 15 will be automatically entered into cells A16 through 20. After we enter five additional donations and set the new cells in the C and D columns to display in money format with two decimal places, our model might appear similar to figure 2.2.

```
A1:                                                          READY

          A            B              C       D      E      F
 1
 2
 3    ITEM #    DESCRIPTION        ESTIMATED MINIMUM
 4                                  VALUE     BID
 5    --------------------------------------------------
 6            1 Green Beret          29.95    5.00
 7            2 Word Processor       99.95   10.00
 8            3 Dinner for 2 at Lees 50.00   25.00
 9            4 1 month at Gents SPA 30.00   10.00
10            5 Melex mens watch     74.95   25.00
11            6 Lady's green scarf   15.00    5.00
12            7 Desk lamp            25.00   12.00
13            8 Walnut bookcase      99.95   15.00
14            9 Desk set             15.00    5.00
15           10 IBM PC Game Disk     34.95   15.00
16           11 Ink well with ink    10.00    2.00
17           12 5 lbs Swiss Cheese   20.00   10.00
18           13 Letter opener         5.00    2.00
19           14 Pen & Pencil Set     10.00    3.00
20           15 Box of Diskettes     20.00   10.00
```

Figure 2.2. Bid Sheet Model after modification

If our auction bid sheet were completed at this time, we would probably want to obtain a listing on our printer and then take this listing to a copy machine to duplicate the number of copies required to provide each person attending the auction with an individual bid sheet. To obtain a listing on the printer we could enter the command:

/Print,Printer,Range,A1.D20◄┘,Go,Page,Quit

which will result in the following camera ready copy that can be duplicated for the auction attendees.

ITEM #	DESCRIPTION	ESTIMATED VALUE	MINIMUM BID
1	Green Beret	29.95	5.00
2	Word Processor	99.95	10.00
3	Dinner for 2 at Lees	50.00	25.00
4	1 month at Gents SPA	30.00	10.00
5	Melex mens watch	74.95	25.00
6	Lady's green scarf	15.00	5.00
7	Desk lamp	25.00	12.00
8	Walnut bookcase	99.95	15.00
9	Desk set	15.00	5.00
10	IBM PC Game Disk	34.95	15.00
11	Ink well with ink	10.00	2.00
12	5 lbs Swiss Cheese	20.00	10.00
13	Letter opener	5.00	2.00
14	Pen & Pencil Set	10.00	3.00
15	Box of Diskettes	20.00	10.00

OTHER MODIFICATIONS TO CONSIDER

Suppose we wish to auction items in sequence based upon their estimated value. We could then use the /DSDP command to sort our auction items based upon their estimated value. To accomplish this, we would enter the command:

/Data,Sort,Data-Range,A6.D20◄┘,Primary-Key,C6◄┘,A◄┘,Go

The preceding command would sort the entries in column C from rows 6 through 20 in ascending sequence. We will still have to change all the item numbers in column A if we wish to renumber them in numerical sequence. This is due to the previous sort causing the item numbers originally assigned to each item being rearranged to correspond to the new sorted sequence by estimated value. Thus, our screen would appear as in figure 2.3 after the /**DSDP** command is entered. Note that the data in column A is resequenced at a value of 1 from row 14. Although this may appear illogical at first glance, an examination of what transpired as a result of the sort will illustrate that this is the expected result. Prior to the sort the data in row 6 contained a 1 in cell A6. When the Green Beret row was moved to row 14 as a result of the sort the value of 1 was placed into cell A14, causing each following cell through cell A20 to have a value one more than the previous cell.

```
A1:                                                                    READY

        A              B                 C        D       E       F
 1
 2
 3   ITEM #      DESCRIPTION         ESTIMATED MINIMUM
 4                                    VALUE     BID
 5   ------------------------------------------------------------
 6           1 Letter opener            5.00    2.00
 7           2 Ink well with ink       10.00    2.00
 8           3 Pen & Pencil Set        10.00    3.00
 9           4 Lady's green scarf      15.00    5.00
10           5 Desk set                15.00    5.00
11           6 5 lbs Swiss Cheese      20.00   10.00
12           7 Box of Diskettes        20.00   10.00
13           8 Desk lamp               25.00   12.00
14           1 Green Beret             29.95    5.00
15           2 1 month at Gents SPA    30.00   10.00
16           3 IBM PC Game Disk        34.95   15.00
17           4 Dinner for 2 at Lees    50.00   25.00
18           5 Melex mens watch        74.95   25.00
19           6 Walnut bookcase         99.95   15.00
20           7 Word Processor          99.95   10.00
```

Figure 2.3. Bid Sheet Model sorted by column C

To resequence the item numbers in column A we would enter 1 into cell A6 and the formula +A6+1 into cell A7. Then, using the /**C** command, we would enter:

/Copy,A7⏎,A8.A20⏎

The preceding copy would place the values 1 through 15 into cells A6 through A20.

Although our model only has 15 entries, suppose our actual auction had several hundred items and the president of our organization called us one evening and asked us what the charity could expect to gross if all items were purchased. By booting up 1-2-3 and loading our model we could enter two @SUM functions to compute the sum of the estimated value and minimum bid columns. Thus, for our previously constructed model we would enter @SUM(C6.C20) into cell C21 and @SUM(D6.D20) into cell D21 to automatically sum the estimated value and minimum bid values of the items on our bid sheet.

The Auctioneer Model

When a large number of persons attend an auction it is customary to give each attendee a bidder number for identification purposes. As each item is sold the auctioneer records the bidder number of the person who purchased the item. To facilitate this process, we can modify our auction bid sheet model by adding a column to enter the bidder number of the purchaser of the item and a column to contain the successful bid offered for the purchase of the item. Thus, using the bid sheet sorted by estimated value we could add the purchaser code and amount headings into columns E and F. This would result in our modified spreadsheet appearing as in figure 2.4.

Prior to actually entering data into the auctioneer model, let us set the formats of columns E and F to reflect the data they will contain. Since the purchaser code is normally an integer, we can enter the following /**RFF** command:

/**R**ange,**F**ormat,**F**ixed,**0**⏎,**E6.E20**⏎

The preceding command will cause the data entered into column E to be displayed right justified as an integer. Since monetary values will be entered into column F, we would use the /**RFF** command to set that column to display data in a money format to include two digits to the right of the decimal point by entering:

/**R**ange,**F**ormat,**F**ixed,**2**⏎,**F6.F20**⏎

```
A1:                                                                      READY

         A              B              C        D       E        F
 1
 2
 3   ITEM #     DESCRIPTION           ESTIMATED MINIMUM PURCHASER
 4                                    VALUE     BID     CODE     AMOUNT
 5   ------------------------------------------------------------------
 6           1 Letter opener             5.00    2.00
 7           2 Ink well with ink        10.00    2.00
 8           3 Pen & Pencil Set         10.00    3.00
 9           4 Lady's green scarf       15.00    5.00
10           5 Desk set                 15.00    5.00
11           6 5 lbs Swiss Cheese       20.00   10.00
12           7 Box of Diskettes         20.00   10.00
13           8 Desk lamp                25.00   12.00
14           9 Green Beret              29.95    5.00
15          10 1 month at Gents SPA     30.00   10.00
16          11 IBM PC Game Disk         34.95   15.00
17          12 Dinner for 2 at Lees     50.00   25.00
18          13 Melex mens watch         74.95   25.00
19          14 Word Processor           99.95   10.00
20          15 Walnut bookcase          99.95   15.00
```

Figure 2.4. The Auctioneer Model

Now that we have adjusted the format of columns E and F to reflect the type of data to be entered, we can save this model under a new file name or simply print it.

If we have a portable computer or desire to transport our computer to the auction site, there are several additional functions we may wish to consider by using 1-2-3. First, many persons do not wait for the auction to end and may wish to leave early. If such persons made several successful bids throughout the evening we could use the /DSDP command to sort our data using the purchaser code as the primary sort key. This will facilitate grouping items according to the purchaser.

Let us assume we took our transportable computer to the auction and keyed in the purchaser code and amount of the winning bid as each item was auctioned. Our completed auctioneer model might then appear as in figure 2.5, assuming the first 15 items were purchased at a certain period in time.

```
A1:                                                                  READY

        A              B              C       D       E      F
1
2
3   ITEM #    DESCRIPTION         ESTIMATED MINIMUM PURCHASER
4                                   VALUE     BID     CODE   AMOUNT
5   ------------------------------------------------------------------
6          1 Letter opener           5.00    2.00      14    15.00
7          2 Ink well with ink      10.00    2.00      12     5.00
8          3 Pen & Pencil Set       10.00    3.00      12     7.50
9          4 Lady's green scarf     15.00    5.00      17    13.00
10         5 Desk set               15.00    5.00      21     7.75
11         6 5 lbs Swiss Cheese     20.00   10.00      14    18.00
12         7 Box of Diskettes       20.00   10.00      19    14.00
13         8 Desk lamp              25.00   12.00      17    20.00
14         9 Green Beret            29.95    5.00      28    22.00
15        10 1 month at Gents SPA   30.00   10.00       2    23.00
16        11 IBM PC Game Disk       34.95   15.00      16    30.00
17        12 Dinner for 2 at Lees   50.00   25.00      18    27.00
18        13 Melex mens watch       74.95   25.00      17    55.00
19        14 Walnut bookcase        99.95   15.00      19    28.75
20        15 Word Processor         99.95   10.00       3    42.00
```

Figure 2.5. Completed Auctioneer Model

Let us assume that at a certain period in time one or more persons wished to leave. Without 1-2-3 or an equivalent spreadsheet program, it could be a long process to determine which items they had purchased. If we were entering data into our auctioneer model, we could use the 1-2-3 **/DSDP** command as follows to sort the data by purchaser code:

/**D**ata,**S**ort,**D**ata-Range,**A6.F20**⏎,**P**rimary-Key,**E6**⏎,**A**⏎,**G**o

Once the sort operation is completed the items will be sorted by purchaser code in ascending sequence. Thus, our auctioneer model would appear as follows:

```
A1:                                                                    READY


        A              B                C        D        E        F
 1
 2
 3   ITEM #    DESCRIPTION          ESTIMATED MINIMUM PURCHASER
 4                                    VALUE     BID     CODE   AMOUNT
 5   -------------------------------------------------------------------
 6         1  1 month at Gents SPA   30.00    10.00        2    23.00
 7         2  Word Processor         99.95    10.00        3    42.00
 8         3  Pen & Pencil Set       10.00     3.00       12     7.50
 9         4  Ink well with ink      10.00     2.00       12     5.00
10         1  Letter opener           5.00     2.00       14    15.00
11         2  5 lbs Swiss Cheese     20.00    10.00       14    18.00
12         3  IBM PC Game Disk       34.95    15.00       16    30.00
13         4  Desk lamp              25.00    12.00       17    20.00
14         5  Melex mens watch       74.95    25.00       17    55.00
15         6  Lady's green scarf     15.00     5.00       17    13.00
16         7  Dinner for 2 at Lees   50.00    25.00       18    27.00
17         8  Box of Diskettes       20.00    10.00       19    14.00
18         9  Walnut bookcase        99.95    15.00       19    28.75
19        10  Desk set               15.00     5.00       21     7.75
20        11  Green Beret            29.95     5.00       28    22.00
```

Notice that the sort operation has again changed the item numbers in column A and we cannot now reference the items by item number.

Suppose bidder number 17 wished to settle his or her account. Based upon the result of the /**DSDP** command, it is easy to see that bidder number 17 purchased 3 items. Although only 3 items were purchased, if we do not have a calculator or wish to double check our math we could enter the 1-2-3 formula @SUM (F13.F15) into cell G15 to compute the amount due from this bidder.

Once the auction is completed it is a simple matter to determine the proceeds of the auction, the revenues actually received and other statistical information that might be desired. Summing the data in the amount column would provide a total of winning bids while summing the entries in column G would show the actual amount received.

From the preceding, it is obvious that 1-2-3 can be both a viable tool to facilitate the preparation of an auction bid sheet as well as to assist in the actual operation of the auction.

3

Checkbook Balancing

Concept

Similar to taxes, balancing one's checkbook is a function that excludes few persons in a modern society. To assist us in keeping an error free record of checking transactions we can use 1-2-3 to develop an electronic model of our checkbook. This model will automatically update our balance as various transactions are entered, and, in addition, provide an electronic record of past transactions since we can save the model to appropriate files that could serve as an indicator of the month and year when those transactions occurred. Thus, a file named JAN85 could be used to indicate our checkbook transactions during January 1985, and so on. Prior to examining the files we can use, let us first construct our basic checkbook model.

Constructing the Model

Since each file we will save after our basic model is developed will represent a month or other increment of time, a time identifier could be included in the model. Here we could simply enter the label PERIOD into column A, row 1, as our entry. Similarly, since each period begins with the prior period's ending balance, we will require a cell in the model into which we will enter the previous balance of our checking account. If we just opened our account, then our initial deposit would be entered into this cell the first time we used the model.

As each transaction consisting of issuing a check or making a deposit causes a new balance to occur in our account, we will require a column to indicate this balance. By an appropriate row entry we can use the BALANCE column to both indicate our previous or initial balance as well as to maintain our running balance as transactions occur. Since we will normally want to set our column headings similar to that of most conventional checkbooks, we will require column headings for the date, check number, a description of the transaction that occurred, deposits and a check amount as well as the previously mentioned balance column.

As the default width of a 1-2-3 column is 9 character positions, we will need to change several column widths to more appropriately reflect the contents they will contain. The following table can be used as a guide for setting the column widths for our checkbook model.

Table 3.1. Checkbook Column Width Assignments

Column	Contents	Width
A	DATE	7
B	CHECK#	6
C	TRANSACTION	20
D	DEPOSIT	9
E	CHECK AMT	9
F	BALANCE	9

We can change the width of the columns by the /**WCS** command. To change the width of column A from its default value of 9 to 7 positions we would move the active cell to any cell in column A and issue the command:

/**W**orksheet,**C**olumn-Width,**S**et,**7**↵

In a similar manner we could change the width of columns B and C. Our initial model with the appropriate column headings entered would appear as follows:

```
F4:                                                                    READY

       A      B          C              D        E        F        G
 1   PERIOD                                              BALANCE
 2                                               PREVIOUS=
 3   DATE    CHECK#   DESCRIPTION      DEPOSIT   CHECK AMT
 4
 5
 6
 7
 8
 9
10
11
12
13
14
15
16
17
18
19
20
```

Since the previous balance will be entered into cell F2, the balance as a result of our first transaction will be +F2+D4-E4. This is because the first transaction will be entered into row 4 and we must add any deposit (D4) to the previous balance (F2) and subtract any check issued (E4) to obtain our current balance. Thus, we will enter the formula +F2+D4-E4 into cell F4.

To see the formulas as they are entered, we should use the /**WGFT** command as follows.

/**W**orksheet,**G**lobal,**F**ormat,**T**ext

For the second transaction which will be entered into row 5, its balance will be the prior balance (F4) plus any deposit (D5) minus any check (E5). Thus, we would enter the formula +F4+D5-E5 into cell F5. Since the balance for each row of transactions is the prior balance plus any deposit and minus any check, we can copy the formula entered into cell F5 downward through column F. The only question that may arise is the depth of the copy through column F.

Since 1-2-3 provides us with 2048 rows, we could copy the formula previously entered into cell F5 from cell F6 through F2048. From a practical viewpoint, most persons fall far short of 2048 transactions during a month and a copy of the formula through cell F2048 would waste a considerable amount of file storage space if we were to save the model several times using filenames reflecting the month and year we wish to use. Assuming 17 transactions are sufficient for most months, we can copy the formula previously entered into cell F5 with the /C command as follows:

/Copy␣F5◄┘F6.F20◄┘

Since the cells in column F are not large enough to display the entire formula, we may increase the width of column F to 16 positions by moving the active cell to any cell in column F and issuing the command:

/Worksheet,Column-Width,Set,16◄┘

As a result of this copy process and the expansion of column F to 16 positions, our model would appear as follows:

```
F1:  'BALANCE                                                          READY

           A       B          C             D       E          F
      1  PERIOD                                              BALANCE
      2                                            PREVIOUS=
      3  DATE    CHECK#    DESCRIPTION      DEPOSIT  CHECK AMT
      4                                                    +F2+D4-E4
      5                                                    +F4+D5-E5
      6                                                    +F5+D6-E6
      7                                                    +F6+D7-E7
      8                                                    +F7+D8-E8
      9                                                    +F8+D9-E9
     10                                                    +F9+D10-E10
     11                                                    +F10+D11-E11
     12                                                    +F11+D12-E12
     13                                                    +F12+D13-E13
     14                                                    +F13+D14-E14
     15                                                    +F14+D15-E15
     16                                                    +F15+D16-E16
     17                                                    +F16+D17-E17
     18                                                    +F17+D18-E18
     19                                                    +F18+D19-E19
     20                                                    +F19+D20-E20
```

It should be noted that if we have a large number of transactions in a particular month we could again use the /C command to continue the copy of the formulas in column F. Thus, although we will save our basic model which only permits 17 transactions, we can easily increase the number of transactions that can be entered into the model.

Transaction Files

Assuming we wish to organize our checkbook model on a monthly basis, we can save the model we just constructed by writing the spreadsheet onto several disk files labeled with appropriate filenames. As an example, suppose we wish to initially create four disk files and label them as JAN85, FEB85, MAR85 and APR85. To save our first file, we would use the /FS command as follows, assuming our data diskette is in the B drive:

/File,Save,B:JAN85⏎

We can use the /FS command several more times to write the model in the computer's memory to additional disk files. In addition, we might wish to save the basic model under the name CHKBOOK or a similar descriptor. Doing so will allow us to use the /FR (File Retrieve) command to load that model and then save it with the /FS command under a different file name. Thus, after we finished using the file APR85, we would be able to load CHKBOOK and save it under the names MAY85, JUN85 and so on.

Using the Model

Since we are dealing with dollars and cents in our checkbook model, we should use the /**WGF** command with the **F** (Fixed) format option to display numbers with two digits after the decimal point. Thus, we would enter:

/Worksheet,Global,Format,Fixed,2↵

When we enter data into the date column, we must insure it is treated as text data by preceding it by a single quotation (') mark. Otherwise, an entry such as 4/02 would result in 1-2-3 dividing 4 by 2. Since we changed the format on a global basis, we must also enter check numbers as text, since, as an example, check number 101 would be stored as 101.00 and result in the display of ****** which serves as an indicator that the number won't fit into the cell. Due to this problem, it might be easier to change only columns D, E and F to the money display option instead of conducting the change on a global basis. Thus, you might consider replacing the global format change with the command:

/Range,Format,Fixed,2↵,D4.F20↵

The preceding command would only place columns D, E and F rows 4 through 20 into the money format display, permitting us to enter check numbers as numeric data instead of text data if we so desired.

Now that we have discussed the model we previously constructed, let us enter sample data into it. Suppose our previous month's balance was $500. We would then enter that amount into cell F2. Next, we would enter each transaction on a separate row until our display might appear similar to figure 3.1.

	A	B	C	D	E	F
						BALANCE
1	PERIOD					
2					PREVIOUS=	500.00
3	DATE	CHECK#	DESCRIPTION	DEPOSIT	CHECK AMT	
4	4/02	100	DONS SERVICE		32.75	467.25
5	4/06		SALARY	600.25		1067.50
6	4/10	101	KARLS MENS SHOPPE		100.77	966.73
7	4/12	102	HERBS DELI DELIGHT		10.00	956.73
8	4/15	103	QUICKIE CLEANERS		35.77	920.96
9	4/18	104	IKES AUTO REPAIR		40.00	880.96
10	4/20	105	BLUE CROSS		50.00	830.96
11	4/20	106	RED CROSS		20.00	810.96
12	4/20		SALARY	600.25		1411.21
13	4/22	107	VISA		325.12	1086.09
14	4/24	108	DELTA AIRLINES		187.43	898.66
15						898.66
16						898.66
17						898.66
18						898.66
19						898.66
20						898.66

Figure 3.1. Checkbook Balancing Model

Note that since we copied the formula in column F through row 20, the balance is carried through cell F20. If we wish to obtain a printout of all transactions that occurred during April, we would most likely want to eliminate rows 15 through 20 as row 14 contained the last transaction that occurred in the month.

To output the relevant portion of our April transactions, we would use the /**PPRGPQ** command as follows:

/**P**rint,**P**rinter,**R**ange,**A1.F14**⏎,**G**o,**P**age,**Q**uit

The result of printing the part of the spreadsheet bounded by cells A1 and F14 is illustrated in figure 3.2.

```
PERIOD                                                 BALANCE
                                        PREVIOUS=      500.00
DATE     CHECK#     DESCRIPTION   DEPOSIT  CHECK AMT
4/02      100 DONS SERVICE                 32.75       467.25
4/06          SALARY            600.25               1067.50
4/10      101 KARLS MENS SHOPPE           100.77       966.73
4/12      102 HERBS DELI DELIGHT           10.00       956.73
4/15      103 QUICKIE CLEANERS             35.77       920.96
4/18      104 IKES AUTO REPAIR            40.00        880.96
4/20      105 BLUE CROSS                   50.00       830.96
4/20      106 RED CROSS                    20.00       810.96
4/20          SALARY            600.25               1411.21
4/22      107 VISA                        325.12      1086.09
4/24      108 DELTA AIRLINES             187.43        898.66
```

Figure 3.2.   Printout of Checkbook Balancing Model

4

Credit Card Recorder

Concept

Since the little pieces of plastic we carry in our wallets have virtually replaced cash in many situations, it is a good idea to record the pertinent information about one's credit cards. Then, in the event the cards are lost or stolen, we can either retrieve the information ourselves or ask a member of our family to do so and contact the appropriate companies that issued the cards to us. Even if we plan to use one of the several firms that specialize in informing credit card issuers of the loss of a client's cards, such firms must first be furnished with a list of cards issued to their clients. In addition, if we should apply for a new credit card or visit our friendly banker to fill out a loan application, we will usually have to enter information concerning the existing credit cards we have. Thus, a credit card recorder model may be a useful data recording tool that can assist us in a variety of situations.

Constructing the Model

Depending upon the ultimate goal of the model, it can be constructed in a variety of ways. If we just desire a simple list of our cards and their numbers, we could simply construct a two-column model to contain the relevant data. In the example that follows, we will use seven columns that should satisfy the data recording requirements of most, if not all, individuals.

Table 4.1 denotes the headings, width and a description of each of the seven columns we will use in our model.

Table 4.1.   Column Format

Column	Heading	Width	Contents
A	CARD	20	Type of card.
B	ISSUER	20	Organization that issued card.
C	ISSUED TO	10	Family member card issued to.
D	ACCOUNT NUMBER	20	Number on card.
E	EXP DATE	10	Date card valid through.
F	TELEPHONE #	14	Number to report lost or stolen card.
G	ADDRESS	35	Where to communicate via mail with credit card issuer.

We can change the width of each column from its default value of 9 to the indicated width in the preceding table by the use of the /**WCS** command. Thus, to change the width of columns A to 20-character positions we would move the active cell to any cell in column A and enter the command:

/**Worksheet,Column-Width,Set,20**⏎

Similarly, we would change the width of columns B through G, using separate /**WCS** commands to change the width of each column.

Once we have formatted the column widths to a sufficient number of positions for most users of this model, we can proceed to enter the headings of the columns across row 1. If we wish to center the heading in each column, we would use the caret (^) character as a prefix to each heading. We should enter a caret (^) and then type CARD into cell A1. In a similar manner we could center the other headings into the remaining six columns.

Assuming we recorded the pertinent information concerning five credit cards issued to our family, let us now obtain a hard copy of this information. Since our model entries will exceed 80 character positions, we must place the printer into a compressed print mode, if it has this capability, in order to print the entire model so that each row of information is contained on one print line.

If our dot matrix printer is capable of printing in a compressed print mode, we can use the /**PPO** command as follows:

/Print,Printer,Options,Setup, \015↵,Margins,Right,136↵,Page-Length,88↵,Quit,Quit

The selection of the **Setup** option allows us to enter a particular setup code which the printer will use to reset itself to compressed mode. The example of **015** is for compressed mode on the IBM Graphics Printer. Since a normal 80 column dot matrix printer is capable of printing 136 characters on a line in compressed print mode, we would change the default right margin to 136 with the **Margins,Right,136** part of the command above. Since compressed mode is also capable of printing 88 lines to a page, we would use the **Page-Length,88** part of the command to increase the page length accordingly.

As a result of the preceding sequence of commands, our model might be printed on the printer in compressed mode with the command:

/Print,Printer,Range,**A1.G6**↵,Go,Page,Quit

The output of this model would appear as follows:

CARD	ISSUER	ISSUED TO	ACCOUNT NUMBER	EXP DATE	TELEPHONE#	ADDRESS
MASTERCARD	GEORGIA SAVINGS	GILBERT	123-456-789	11/86	912-477-XXXX	4777 LOAN WAY MACON, GA 31210
VISA	GEORGIA SAVINGS	BEVERLY	123-456-789	12/87	912-477-XXXX	4777 LOAN WAY MACON, GA 31210
AMERICAN EXPRESS	AMERICAN EXPRESS	GILBERT	123-456-789	5/85	212-XXX-XXXX	DONT LEAVE HOME LANE, NY NY
EATERS CLUB	DIET CORPORATION	BEVERLY	123-456-789	7/88	516-756-XXXX	12 HONEY CT DIET CITY, NY
AT&T	AT&T	GILBERT	912-XXX-XXXX-XXX	2/86	912-XXX-XXXX	77 TOLL WAY MACON, GA 31210

To facilitate the updating of this model, we should save it prior to moving on to our next model. Thus, we could enter the command:

/File,Save,B:CREDIT⏎

if we wish to save this model under the filename CREDIT on the diskette in drive B.

5

The Food Shopping List

Concept

Like many things in life, food shopping is a routine some of us prefer to put off until the last possible moment. Unfortunately, doing so usually results in the omission of one or more products as well as the purchase of many unnecessary items during our sojourn up and down the aisles of the neighborhood grocery store.

Although many persons write a shopping list, the list may only alleviate a portion of potential food shopping problems. This results from the fact that it is far easier to open the refrigerator and cabinet doors to write a list of items we are low on or immediately note by their absence than to methodically consider whether or not we need any of the hundred of items we may normally purchase. Usually in our rush to the food store we may fail to consider one or more items we used up several days ago or the special item our spouse or children requested, resulting in a second trip to the monument of modern civilization.

By using our spreadsheet, we can develop a comprehensive food shopping list that can serve as a memory jogger when we look through our cabinets and refrigerator. Similar to the attendance list we previouly created, we can place a pair of brackets next to each entry that will allow us to simply check those items we wish to purchase. Once we develop our model, we can generate several copies of the shopping list on our printer or duplicate copies of one printout on a copying machine. In addition, once we save our basic model, we can add additional entries and eventually tailor the shopping list to our budget and taste buds.

Constructing the Model

Since the food purchasing habits of families can differ significantly, the model we will construct should be viewed as a guide for the development of a shopping list to satisfy one's particular budget, taste and family circumstance.

Assuming we wish to enter the items we normally purchase based upon the section of the store where they are located our initial model might appear as follows:

```
A1:  'BAKERY                                                              READY

           A           B           C           D        E        F        G        H
1    BAKERY                              MILK/CHEESE
2      White bread                         1gal Low fat
3      Rye bread                           1gal regular
4      Bagels                              Cream cheese
5      Rolls                               Cottage cheese
6    CEREALS                               Muenster
7      Cold                                Swiss
8      Hot                               POULTRY
9    FRUIT                                 Chicken legs
10     Apples                              Chicken breasts
11     Bananas                           SNACK FOOD
12     Cantalope                           Ice cream
13     Kiwi                                Low calorie soda
14   MEATS                                 Mixed nuts
15     Chops                               Pretzels
16     Flank Steak                         Taco chips
17     Rib Roast                         SODA
18     Veal                                Cola
19
20
```

In the preceding example, we entered the items we normally purchase based upon their location in the food store. Note that to obtain a one-space indentation of each item under its appropriate section heading, we must enter the item as text data preceded by a space. Although we entered our data into two columns, one could enter the data into a single column, three columns or some other format to suit one's preference.

Since the length of the longest item entered into column A is 12 character positions, for clarity we can set the width of column A to 13 positions by moving the active cell to any cell in column A and entering the command:

/**W**orksheet,**C**olumn-Width,**S**et,**13**↵

As a result of entering this command for columns A and D, our model would appear on our screen as follows.

```
A1:  'BAKERY                                                              READY

            A          B          C            D          E        F        G
  1   BAKERY                              MILK/CHEESE
  2    White bread                         1gal Low fat
  3    Rye bread                           1gal regular
  4    Bagels                              Cream cheese
  5    Rolls                               Cottage cheese
  6   CEREALS                              Muenster
  7    Cold                                Swiss
  8    Hot                                POULTRY
  9   FRUIT                                Chicken legs
 10    Apples                              Chicken breasts
 11    Bananas                            SNACK FOOD
 12    Cantalope                           Ice cream
 13    Kiwi                                Low calorie soda
 14   MEATS                                Mixed nuts
 15    Chops                               Pretzels
 16    Flank Steak                         Taco chips
 17    Rib Roast                          SODA
 18    Veal                                Cola
 19
 20
```

Now we can enter a pair of brackets into cells B1 and F1 and copy the bracket pairs through row 18 of each column. Once the pair of brackets is entered into cell B1, we would enter the command:

/**C**opy,**B1**↵,**B2.B18**↵

This command would cause the pair of brackets previously entered into cell B1 to be copied from cell B2 through B18. Similarly we would enter the command:

/Copy,F1⏎,F2.F18⏎

to copy the pair of brackets through cell 18 of column F. Our model would appear as follows:

```
B1: '[   ]                                                                  READY

              A            B        C           D           E          F          G
    1   BAKERY        [   ]              MILK/CHEESE              [   ]
    2     White bread [   ]                1gal Low fat           [   ]
    3     Rye bread   [   ]                1gal regular           [   ]
    4     Bagels      [   ]                Cream cheese           [   ]
    5     Rolls       [   ]                Cottage cheese         [   ]
    6   CEREALS       [   ]                Muenster               [   ]
    7     Cold        [   ]                Swiss                  [   ]
    8     Hot         [   ]              POULTRY                  [   ]
    9   FRUIT         [   ]                Chicken legs           [   ]
   10     Apples      [   ]                Chicken breasts        [   ]
   11     Bananas     [   ]              SNACK FOOD               [   ]
   12     Cantalope   [   ]                Ice cream              [   ]
   13     Kiwi        [   ]                Low calorie soda       [   ]
   14   MEATS         [   ]                Mixed nuts             [   ]
   15     Chops       [   ]                Pretzels               [   ]
   16     Flank Steak [   ]                Taco chips             [   ]
   17     Rib Roast   [   ]              SODA                     [   ]
   18     Veal        [   ]                Cola                   [   ]
   19
   20
```

We can enter the command:

/Print,Printer,Range,A1.F18⏎,Go,Page,Quit

to obtain a printed listing of our model which we can duplicate on a copying machine or we can simply print as many copies of our shopping list as we feel we require.

Modifications to Consider

Although we might spend a considerable length of time developing a comprehensive shopping list, the chances are excellent that we will omit one or more items which upon occasion we will want to purchase. Taking this fact into consideration, we could add several unlabeled lines to our model and perhaps tape the model to our refrigerator door. This would allow us to easily add items to our list as the requirement materializes and we could also update our model on a periodic basis to add such items to our shopping list. Thus, after our initial list is developed, we should use the /**FS** (File,Save) command to save our model, facilitating its modification if the requirement materializes.

6

Mailing Label Generator

Concept

One of the most common characteristics of civic organizations is the need for the mailing of a newsletter or brochure on a periodic basis. Due to the ability of 1-2-3 to output the contents of a range of cells to a printer, we can construct a file of names and addresses of persons in our organization. Then, each time we need to mail a brochure or newsletter, we can use 1-2-3 to output the contents of our spreadsheet onto peelable, self-adhesive labels. This will permit us to peel off the printed labels and affix them onto our organization's brochure or newsletter, eliminating the repetitive process of typing the names and addresses of members onto such labels for each mailing.

Constructing the Model

The first item we must consider prior to constructing our model is the size of the labels we will use. The label size is most important as it will govern where we place the names and addresses of members of our organization within the spreadsheet.

Let us assume that the labels we will use are capable of holding 8 lines of print, with each line capable of containing up to 40 characters of data. Thus, the dimension of our labels in terms of their printing capacity might be visually displayed as in figure 6.1.

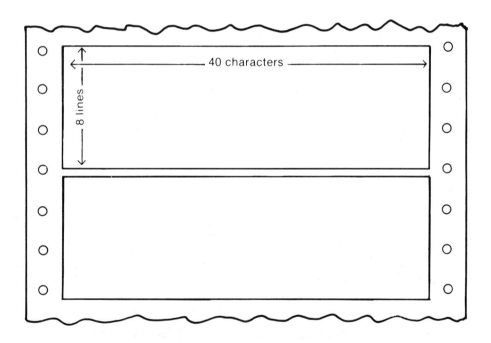

Figure 6.1.   Label printing capacity

Since the labels we will use have the capacity to hold up to 40 characters per printed line, our printed labels would look awkward unless we attempt to center the names and addresses on each label. If we assume that the maximum number of characters in a member's name is 25, we will require (40-25)/2 or 7 or 8 positions to be blank prior to printing the member's name on the label. Similarly, if the typical member of our organization has a 2-line address we would require 3 lines to be printed on the label to include the line containing their name. Since each label can hold 8 printed lines, we would commence printing on either line 3 or 4 of the label to center the name and address.

In constructing our model, we will use only 5 members for simplicity, although the basic concepts can be used to create a mailing list of hundreds of members. Since we could commence printing on either line 3 or 4 of the first label, we will commence entering our data in row 3 of our model. If the name and address consists of 3 lines of text, we will skip 3 rows to reach the end of the label and 2 more rows to reach the near center position of the next label. Thus, we must skip 5 rows after entering the first member's name and address prior to entering the next member's name and address. Then, we would continue this process of skipping 5 rows and entering the next member's name and address on 3 rows until we reach row 2048 which is the bottom of the column. Since we require 8 lines per label, we can place 256 (2048/8) member names and addresses into one column and print the contents from row 1 through row 2048 onto 256 labels. If our membership list exceeds 256, we could use additional columns for each additional group of 256 or less members. Since 1-2-3 provides us with 256 columns, we could theoretically develop a mailing list file containing the names and addresses of 65,536 members. For the majority of civic organizations, this capacity should be more than sufficient, however, one could save names and addresses on multiple files if one file should prove insufficient in capacity.

Returning to the construction of our model, let us move the active cell to any cell in column A and use the /**WCS** command to set the width of column A to 25 positions as follows:

/**W**orksheet,**C**olumn-Width,**S**et,**25**⤶

Now, let us enter 5 names and addresses whose relation to reality is fictitious but will serve to illustrate the concept of printing mailing labels. After entering the data, we will use the /**PPR** command to verify the position of each entry in column A. The result of the command:

/**P**rint,**P**rinter,**R**ange,**A1.A37**⤶,**G**o,**P**age,**Q**uit

is shown in figure 6.2.

```
Mr. Herbert Harris
4736 Oxford Road
Anytown, Ga. 31210




Mr. Dingle Bat
4727 Ohvey Circle
Atlanta, Ga. 31110




Mr. & Mrs. Soda Pop
9988 Ridge Road
Macon, Ga. 31211




Mr. Fife Drummer
12 Soundaway Circle
Gaineshaven, Ga. 32212




Dr. Donna Devine
38 Kadoodle Ave., Apt 37
Macon, Ga. 31210
```

Figure 6.2.   Result of the /PPR command

Suppose we desired to print five labels using the names and addresses previously entered into our model. Since we will print the contents of cells A1 through A37, printing will commence in character position 1 on each label. This will obviously not center the name and address on each label.

If we wish to center the names and addresses on each label we must consider the number of print positions on each label as well as the maximum number of characters that can be entered in a cell to represent a name or address. As our labels are assumed to have the capacity to hold 40 characters per line and the cell width only allows 25 character positions, we should commence printing in character position (40-25)/2 to center each name and address on a line.

Two methods can be considered to commence printing of names and addresses in position 8 on each label line. If we have a printer that allows us to set the left print margin we could use the /**PPOML** command as follows:

/**P**rint,**P**rinter,**O**ptions,**M**argin,**L**eft,**8**⏎,**Q**uit,**G**o,**P**age,**Q**uit

This would cause 1-2-3 to print the names and addresses in column A onto the labels, with printing commencing in column 8 on each label.

If our printer's left margin cannot be set we can still use 1-2-3 to basically perform the same function as printing labels from position 8 onward. To do this, we would first use the following /**M** command to move the contents of column A into column B.

/**M**ove,**A1.A37**,⏎,**B1.B37**⏎

After the data from column A is moved into column B, column B will have a width of 8 positions while A will still have a width of 25 positions. We can set the width of column A to 7 positions and the width of column B to 25 positions by moving the active cell to any cell in the column we wish to set the width of, and using the /**WCS** commands as follows:

/**W**orksheet,**C**olumn-Width,**S**et,**7**⏎
/**W**orksheet,**C**olumn-Width,**S**et,**25**⏎

The two preceding commands will result in the data in column B being printed in position 8 when we use the **Range,A1.B37** in a /**PP** command. Thus, the command:

/**P**rint,**P**rinter,**R**ange,**A1.B37**⏎,**G**o,**P**age,**Q**uit

would result in the following printout.

```
Mr. Herbert Harris
4736 Oxford Road
Anytown, Ga. 31210




Mr. Dingle Bat
4727 Ohvey Circle
Atlanta, Ga. 31110




Mr. & Mrs. Soda Pop
9988 Ridge Road
Macon, Ga. 31211




Mr. Fife Drummer
12 Soundaway Circle
Gaineshaven, Ga. 32212




Dr. Donna Devine
38 Kadoodle Ave., Apt 37
Macon, Ga. 31210
```

Prior to discussing an option that can be used to automate the issuing of commands, let us restore our model to its original form where the names and addresses were entered into column A and column B's width was 9 positions. This is accomplished by issuing the following /**M** and /**WCS** commands:

/Move,**B1.B37**↵,**A1.A37**↵
/**W**orksheet,**C**olumn-Width,**S**et,**9**↵
/**W**orksheet,**C**olumn-Width,**S**et,**25**↵

Be sure to move the active cell to any cell in the column we are setting the width of.

Now, let us save the model using the following /**FS** command.

/**File**,**Save**,**B:MAILLIST**↵

The execution of the preceding command will save the entire file on disk under the filename MAILLIST with the extension .WKS on the diskette in drive B.

Automating the Process

Once we complete the entry of a large number of names and addresses into a model it could become a laborious process to issue the commands necessary to print the required labels. This is because we would have to issue separate /**PPRGPQ** commands for each pair of columns if we were using labels one across.

To facilitate the label printing process, we can fill a range of cells with the sequence of 1-2-3 commands required to perform the desired operations. This range can be named with the /**R**ange,**N**ame command and is called a MACRO. Then, we could load our file of names and addresses and use the MACRO to automatically perform the operations necessary to print the labels.

To create a MACRO from 1-2-3, we must enter each command sequence of key strokes as text into a cell in the worksheet. Then we can save the commands to a worksheet file.

To see how we can use the MACRO command, let us assume we wish to automatically perform the following operations upon the data in the file named MAILLIST.WKS.

OPERATIONS TO BE PERFORMED AUTOMATICALLY

- Move the data in column A to column B.
- Set the width of column A to 7 positions.
- Output the contents of cell A1 through B38 to the printer.

To perform the preceding operations automatically, we would create an execute MACRO from 1-2-3 by entering the necessary commands as text into a cell of the spreadsheet model. Thus, let us first use the /**RE** command to erase or empty the range in the spreadsheet where we will store our commands by entering:

/Range,Erase,**C1.C20**⏎

Now, let us enter the commands necessary to perform the three operations previously indicated. Note that each line in the execute file must contain only those characters we would press on the keyboard to execute a specific command. Thus, we would enter '/ MA1.A37~B1.B37~ into cell C1 which are the command characters necessary to move column A to column B. Next, we would enter '{HOME} / WCS7~ into cell C2 to move the active cell to column A and set the width of column A to 7 positions. Finally, we would enter '/ PPRA1.B38~GPQ into cell C3 which will cause the contents of cells A1 through B38 to be printed. Thus, the commands we will save should appear on our screen as illustrated on the following page.

We must now assign a special keystroke name to the three cells containing the MACRO. Using the command:

/Range,Name,Create, \P⏎,C1⏎

will name our MACRO so that it can be executed by simply holding down the [ALT] Key and pressing the letter P.

Now, let us save the commands using the /**FS** command as follows:

/File,Save,**B:MAILLIST**⏎

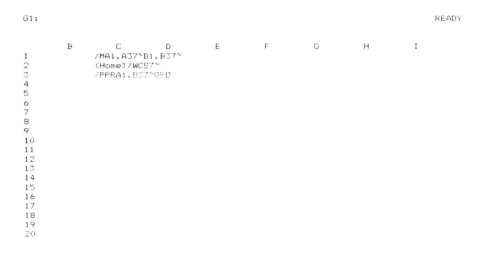

The preceding command will save the commands and worksheet previously entered onto the file named MAILLIST with the extension .WKS on the diskette in drive B. Once the contents of MAILLIST.WKS are loaded, we can execute the three commands stored in the spreadsheet by entering the MACRO as follows:

Alt P   (hold down the [Alt] key and press P)

Although the preceding may appear to be a considerable effort to automate three commands, its value increases as the number of names and addresses in our MAILLIST file increases. This is because the use of two or more columns to contain our names and addresses will increase the number of commands we will have to enter each time we wish to print a set of labels and the execute command will eventually become a significant mechanism to reduce command sequence entries.

7

Telephone Directory

Concept

Although the personal computer does not replace the convenience of pocket sized or desktop telephone directories, through the use of a spreadsheet model one can obtain a large degree of flexibility in creating, updating and printing telephone directory information. Since one of the requirements of most civic organizations is to have an up-to-date telephone directory of members, a spreadsheet can be used most advantageously in this area.

Constructing the Model

Suppose our Boy Scout troop currently has 10 members and we wish to use 1-2-3 to prepare a telephone directory of our members. If we wish to include the last name, first name, middle initial and telephone number of each member of the troop in our directory we will require four columns in our model to contain the relevant data.

From an investigation of the length of member names, let us assume we determined that a maximum of 11 positions will be required for one's last name and 9 positions for one's first name. Since we will wish to separate the last and first names for clarity of display, we would therefore require a column of 12 character positions for the last name and 10 positions for the first name. To separate one's middle initial from one's telephone number we might require a column 3 positions wide to contain a middle initial followed by a period. If all members of the troop have the same area code we might decide that the default column width of 9 positions is sufficient to contain the telephone number of each member.

Based upon the preceding, let us assume our column assignments and columns widths will be as indicated in table 7.1.

Table 7.1. Telephone Directory column assignments

Column	Data	Width
A	Last Name	12
B	First Name	10
C	Middle Initial	3
D	Telephone Number	9

To change the column widths we will move the active cell to the appropriate column and use the /**WCS** command three times as column D need not be changed. Our entries to change the width of columns A, B and C would be:

```
/Worksheet,Column-Width,Set,12↵
/Worksheet,Column-Width,Set,10↵
/Worksheet,Column-Width,Set,3↵
```

Let us now position the cursor at cell A1 and enter the text label **TROOP #007 Telephone Directory** into that cell. Now let us skip to row 3 and begin to enter member names and their telephone numbers. Although we can enter telephone numbers as 7 digit integers, for clarity of display we will probably enter this data as text information and include a dash (-) between the third and fourth digit of each number sequence. Thus, the telephone number 7454433 would be entered '745-4433 to denote to 1-2-3 that it is text.

After entering our heading information and sample data, our telephone directory model might appear as follows:

```
A13:                                                              READY

          A          B         C    D        E        F        G        H
 1   Troop #007 Telephone Directory
 2
 3   Doebell      Frankie    Z.  477-0293
 4   Smith        Howard     K.  744-2048
 5   Kravits      Sammie         743-1234
 6   James        Herbert    Q.  743-2222
 7   Kitchens     Cleanie    M.  745-1222
 8   Able         Ronald     R.  745-4433
 9   Zapata       Emile      G.  747-7071
10   Marshall     Tomas      T.  743-7777
11   Lamarmore    Melvin     F.  743-9888
12   Devine       Dona           745-9876
13
14
15
16
17
18
19
20
```

Let us assume that we entered our data from a list furnished to us during a meeting and therefore did not alphabetize our membership list. While we could have taken the time to place our members' names into alphabetical order prior to entering them into our model, we can avoid this manual alphabetization process since 1-2-3 has a /**DS** command which can be used to automatically place our list into an alphabetically sorted order.

Suppose we wish to sort our telephone directory based upon the last name of each member. Since the last names of members are contained in cells A3 through A12, we would use the /**DS** command as follows.

/Data,Sort,Data-Range,**A3.D12**↵,Primary-Key,**A3**↵,**A**↵,Go

Here the **A3** entered after **Primary-Key** indicates to 1-2-3 that the sort is to be performed on column A. The entry **A3.D12** denotes that rows 3 through 12 in columns A through D are to be sorted while the last **A** entered signifies that the sort is to be performed in ascending sequence. Once the /**DS** command is executed, our telephone directory model would be in sorted alphabetical order with the sort based upon the last names of the members in Troop #007 and would appear as follows:

```
A13:                                                              READY

           A          B          C     D       E      F      G      H
 1    Troop #007 Telephone Directory
 2
 3    Able       Ronald     R. 745-4433
 4    Devine     Dona          745-9876
 5    Doebell    Frankie    Z. 477-0293
 6    James      Herbert    Q. 743-2222
 7    Kitchens   Cleanie    M. 745-1222
 8    Kravits    Sammie        743-1234
 9    Lamarmore  Melvin     F. 743-8888
10    Marshall   Tomas      T. 743-7777
11    Smith      Howard     K. 744-2048
12    Zapata     Emile      G. 747-7071
13
14
15
16
17
18
19
20
```

After our telephone directory is complete, we will probably want a printed copy which we could then duplicate in sufficient quantity to provide a copy to each member of the troop.

To obtain a printed copy of our directory we would use the /**PPR** command as follows:

/Print,Printer,Range,**A1.D12**↵,Go,Page,Quit

As a result of the /**PPR** command, our telephone directory printout would appear as follows:

```
Troop #007 Telephone Directory

Able          Ronald      R.  745-4433
Devine        Dona            745-9876
Doebell       Frankie     Z.  477-0293
James         Herbert     Q.  743-2222
Kitchens      Cleanie     M.  745-1222
Kravits       Sammie          743-1234
Lamarmore     Melvin      F.  743-8888
Marshall      Tomas       T.  743-7777
Smith         Howard      K.  744-2048
Zapata        Emile       G.  747-7071
```

If we have no changes at this time, we should consider saving our model as this will facilitate any updating that may be required in the future. If our 1-2-3 diskette is in drive A and a data diskette is in drive B, we could save our model onto the data diskette by using the /**FS** command as follows:

/File,Save,**B:TELDIR**⏎

The preceding command will cause the contents of our telephone directory model to be saved on the file named TELDIR on the diskette in drive B.

Modifying the Directory

Let us assume that a new member of Troop #007 appeared at our next meeting and we wish to revise our telephone directory to bring it up to date. Once we return home we can use 1-2-3 to retrieve our directory model which was previously stored under the filename TELDIR by using the /**FR** command as follows:

/File,Retrieve,**B:TELDIR**⏎

Let us assume we wish to add Martin A. Kruger, whose telephone number is 745-7766, to our directory. Since our directory ended in row 12, we could position the active cell to A13 and enter the information and then use the /**DS** command to resort our list. Another option would be to open a row for the insertion of data for Mr. Kruger by using the /**WIR** command. Since Kruger follows Kravits, we would insert a row at row 9 using the /**WIR** command as follows:

/Worksheet,Insert,Row,**A9**⌐

Next, we would enter the data for Mr. Kruger and our telephone directory would appear as follows:

```
D14:                                                          READY

         A          B         C    D       E      F       G        H
1   Troop #007 Telephone Directory
2
3   Able       Ronald    R.  745-4433
4   Devine     Dona          745-9876
5   Doebell    Frankie   Z.  477-0293
6   James      Herbert   O.  743-2222
7   Kitchens   Cleanie   M.  745-1222
8   Kravits    Sammie        743-1234
9   Kruger     Martin    A.  745-7766
10  Lamarmore  Melvin    F.  743-8888
11  Marshall   Tomas     T.  743-7777
12  Smith      Howard    K.  744-2048
13  Zapata     Emile     G.  747-7071
14
15
16
17
18
19
20
```

With only one addition to the directory the difference in time between appending entries and rearranging them in alphabetical order by using the /**DS** command or inserting a row by using the /**WIR** command is insignificant. If we have many additions to our directory, it would be much faster to first append these entries after the last previously entered row and then use the /**DS** command to place the directory into sorted order.

Now that our directory is updated we can obtain a new listing on our printer. Once again, we can use the /**PPR** command to obtain our listing. Since our model is now contained in the area bounded by cells A1 to D13, the /**PPR** command would be entered as follows:

/Print,Printer,Range,**A1.D13**⌐,Go,Page,Quit

The /**PPR** command would result in the printing of the updated telephone directory listing which follows:

```
Troop #007 Telephone Directory

   Able         Ronald    R.  745-4433
   Devine       Dona          745-9876
   Doebell      Frankie   Z.  477-0293
   James        Herbert   Q.  743-2222
   Kitchens     Cleanie   M.  745-1222
   Kravits      Sammie        743-1234
   Kruger       Martin    A.  745-7766
   Lamarmore    Melvin    F.  743-8888
   Marshall     Tomas     T.  743-7777
   Smith        Howard    K.  744-2048
   Zapata       Emile     G.  747-7071
```

Since we previously saved our telephone directory using the filename TELDIR, upon entering the command, /**File,Save,B:TELDIR**⏎, the prompt message "Cancel, Replace" would appear. To save the current version of TELDIR that is currently in memory onto the diskette we would respond to the prompt by entering the letter R. This will replace the old version on disk with the current version in memory.

Constraints

The major constraint for an automated telephone directory is the number of persons that can be included in the model. Since 1-2-3 has 2048 rows, we could have up to 2048 entries if we were willing to forego the use of a heading. If our membership list exceeds 2048, we can simply use another set of columns in our spreadsheet. Thus, we might change column E to a width of 2 or 3 positions to serve as a divider between pairs of columns and then use columns F through I similar to the manner we used columns A through D.

8

Stamp Collecting

Concept

Stamp collectors perform many functions that are suitable for incorporation into one or more spreadsheet models. Foremost among these functions are the development of a wantlist and an inventory or collection valuation.

A stamp collector's wantlist, as the name implies, is a listing of stamps that one requires to complete his or her collection. Typically, the list references catalogue numbers contained in one of the major stamp collector catalogues, such as the *Scott Postage Stamp Catalogue*. Although Scott is considered the bible of philately, there are many other postage stamp catalogues upon which one may wish to base his or her wantlist. Thus, wantlists usually indicate the catalogue used to avoid potential misunderstandings. Since many collectors have specialized into collecting plate blocks, first day covers and other narrowly defined areas, one may also wish to describe specifically what he or she requires. Once the wantlist is completed, it can easily be updated as items are added to one's collection. An additional benefit from having a wantlist constructed as a spreadsheet model is the ease in printing the spreadsheet which can then be mailed to dealers or carried by the collector to stamp shows and collector bourses to facilitate obtaining the items one requires.

Although few persons have the economic resources to build an award-winning stamp collection, one's collection can considerably increase in value due to inflation and additions added to the collection over a number of years. Since most homeowner insurance policies only provide coverage for the first $500 of the value of a stamp collection, a separate rider is normally required to insure one's stamp collection. While your insurance company may require you to obtain a professional appraisal, you can facilitate that appraisal process by constructing a spreadsheet collection valuation model. In general, this model should list the items in your collection by referencing an appropriate stamp collector catalogue number and identifying the catalogue value of each item. Since catalogue values are assigned on an annual basis while stamps like all commodities fluctuate in value on a daily basis based upon supply and demand, you may also wish to indicate the market value of each item in your collection. This can be accomplished by reading one of the many weekly or monthly stamp publications and denoting the retail price listed by dealers for the items you have in your collection.

The Wantlist Model

If you plan to mail your wantlist to dealers you may wish to include your name, address and perhaps your telephone number in your wantlist. If the purpose of your wantlist is to obtain an up-to-date, easily modified list you wish to carry in your wallet, you can obviously exclude this type of information from the list.

For the wantlist model we will develop, let us assume that we collect both unused and used United States airmail stamps. Since very few stamp collectors remember the association between a catalogue number and a particular stamp, we may wish to include a description column in our spreadsheet model to assist in identifying the stamp. Two other columns we can include would be an unused column and a used column. By placing an appropriate marker in each column we can use that marker to indicate whether or not we need an unused or used copy of the stamp. While the word NEED or an asterisk (*) might be the most common types of markers to employ, one can also consider placing the catalogue value or retail price of the particular item in the appropriate column corresponding to the item's catalogue number. Doing so will allow you to use the capability of the spreadsheet to sum up the values of each column and instantly note the total catalogue value or retail price of those items missing from the collection.

The Checkoff Model

Our first wantlist model is also known as a checkoff list. In this model, we employ four columns to denote those unused and used stamps that are missing from our U.S. airmail collection. Here we will place the word NEED in each column on the appropriate row that defines the stamp's catalogue number to indicate it is missing from our collection. When we send a printed copy of the model to a stamp dealer or search for the items at stamp exhibitions, we can simply mark a check through the word NEED to denote we have obtained a copy of the required item. Then, when time permits we can update our model to remove those items from our wantlist that we have obtained. Let us first enter the headings required by our model, perhaps resulting in our spreadsheet appearing as follows:

```
A8:                                                           READY

        A        B         C         D         E        F        G        H
 1   WANTLIST FOR US AIRMAIL STAMPS AS OF 4/1/85
 2
 3   CONTACT:  JOHN DOE            912/xxx-xxxx
 4             45 Collectors Way
 5             Anytown, USA
 6
 7   SCOTT #  DESCRIPTION          UNUSED    USED
 8
 9
10
11
12
13
14
15
16
17
18
19
20
```

Since airmail stamps' catalogue numbers are prefixed by the letter C, we would enter C1 into cell A8 if we need Scott catalogue number C1.

After completing our wantlist, let us assume it appears as follows:

```
E14:                                                          READY

        A        B         C         D         E        F        G        H
 1   WANTLIST FOR US AIRMAIL STAMPS AS OF 4/1/85
 2
 3   CONTACT:  JOHN DOE            912/xxx-xxxx
 4             45 Collectors Way
 5             Anytown, USA
 6
 7   SCOTT #  DESCRIPTION          UNUSED    USED
 8   C1       6c Jenny                       NEED
 9   C14      1.30 Zeppelin        NEED      NEED
10   C15      2.60 Zeppelin        NEED      NEED
11   C18      50c Graf Zeppelin              NEED
12   C31      50c Twin Motor                 NEED
13   C46      80c Hawaii                     NEED
14
15
16
17
18
19
20
```

Now if we enter the command:

/Print,Printer,Range,A1.E13⏎,Go,Page,Quit

our wantlist would be printed as follows:

```
WANTLIST FOR US AIRMAIL STAMPS AS OF 4/1/85

CONTACT: JOHN DOE          912/xxx-xxxx
         45 Collectors Way
         Anytown, USA

SCOTT #  DESCRIPTION        UNUSED    USED
C1       6c Jenny                     NEED
C14      1.30 Zeppelin      NEED      NEED
C15      2.60 Zeppelin      NEED      NEED
C18      50c Graf Zeppelin            NEED
C31      50c Twin Motor               NEED
C46      80c Hawaii                   NEED
```

Since new issues and the purchase of stamps we require will alter our wantlist, we should save this model if we wish to update it in the future. Thus, entering the command:

/File,Save,B:USAIR⏎

would save our wantlist model under the filename USAIR on the diskette in drive B.

Let us assume that at a later date we finally purchase a used and unused copy of Scott #C15. If we want to update our wantlist we could first load our file and then use the /**WDR** command to delete row 10 from our model. Thus, we would enter the command:

/File,Retrieve,B:USAIR⏎

to our wantlist model and then enter the command:

/Worksheet,Delete,Row,A10⏎

to delete the entry concerning Scott catalogue number C15. After printing a new wantlist we should update our diskfile by resaving the model in memory that was just updated. Thus, we would enter the letter R to specify Replace when we enter the /**FS** command to save our file.

The Inventory Model

The purpose of the inventory or collection valuation model is to develop a record of the items in our collection. We can tailor this model in many ways depending upon the information we wish to enter into our model. Like the previously covered wantlist model, we can define the subject of our collection, the catalogue used for reference purposes and a number of columns in the spreadsheet to correspond to the type of items in our collection. Let us assume we collect unused and used United States airmail stamps. However, for simplicity, we will only consider 10 Scott issues in our collection. The following model illustrates how we could construct our inventory. Note that we entered the command:

/**R**ange,Format,Fixed,**2**⏎,**D4.E17**⏎

to display the catalogue values of items in our collection in a money format with 2 digits after the decimal point.

```
D17:  (F2) +D15+E15                                                    READY

            A         B          C          D        E         F       G       H
    1                 US AIRMAIL COLLECTION INVENTORY AS OF 5/01/85
    2
    3     SCOTT #  DESCRIPTION           UNUSED    USED
    4     C1       6c Jenny              175.00
    5     C2       16c Jenny             225.00    52.50
    6     C3       24c Jenny             225.00    60.00
    7     C4       8c Propeller           65.00    22.50
    8     C5       16c Emblem            225.00    50.00
    9     C6       24c De Havilland      275.00    40.00
   10     C7       10c Map                 6.50     0.50
   11     C8       15c Map                 7.00     2.75
   12     C9       20c Map                22.50     2.25
   13     C10      10c Lindberg           16.00     3.00
   14                                  ------------------
   15                                   1242.00   233.50
   16
   17     TOTAL CATALOGUE VALUE:        1475.50
   18
   19
   20
```

To accumulate the total value of the unused and used stamps in our collection, we would simply enter the function @SUM(D4.D13) into cell D14 and the function @SUM(E4.E13) into cell E14. We have also indicated the total catalogue value of our collection by entering the formula +D15+E15 into cell D17 in the preceding example. If we wish to send our list to the insurance company we would print our inventory. Thus, we would enter the command:

/Print,Printer,Range,**A1.E17**⏎,**Go**,**Page**,**Quit**

to print our inventory model. Then we would save our model since we will normally update it each year to reflect the changes in the catalogue value of our collection.

Modifications to Consider

Those persons who consider stamp collecting to be both a hobby and an investment may wish to use a spreadsheet model not only to place a value on their collection but, in addition, to compute the percent change in the value of the items in the collection from one year to another. To see how this can be accomplished, let us examine an inventory model containing just a few items for simplicity. Then once we see how to construct this model we can apply its principles to additional items we may have in our collection.

The structure of the model to contain the data elements required to determine the percentage change in the catalogue value of items in a collection might appear as illustrated on the following page.

Since we will most likely prefer a money display format in column B, C and E, we would enter the commands:

/Range,Format,Fixed,**2**⏎,**B1.C100**⏎
/Range,Format,Fixed,**2**⏎,**E1.E100**⏎

to display data entered in these columns with 2 decimal digits.

By employing two columns to record the catalogue value of stamps in the collection for 1984 and 1985, we will have the appropriate data necessary to compute the percentage change in catalogue value of each

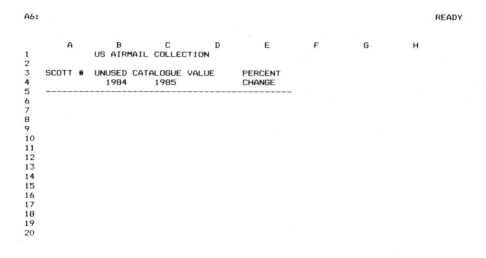

stamp in the collection. The percentage change can be computed as follows:

$$\text{Percent Change} = \left(\frac{1985 \text{ value} - 1984 \text{ value}}{1984 \text{ value}}\right) * 100$$

Although the preceding formula is straightforward, suppose we added an item to the collection during 1985. Then, since no value would be associated with the stamp for 1984, the preceding formula would result in a division by zero which would cause 1-2-3 to generate the message ERR. To avoid this error message we could enter the formula:

@IF(B6<=0,0,(((C6-B6/B6)*100))

into cell E6. This would cause the number 0 to be displayed if we did not have the item in our collection during the preceding year. The following partial display of our model indicates the formula entry required in cells E6 and E7 necessary to suppress an error message if we did not have an item in the collection during the preceding year.

```
E6:  (T)  @IF(B6<=0,0,(((C6-B6)/B6)*100))                                    READY

         A         B         C         D                  E
 1                 US AIRMAIL COLLECTION
 2
 3       SCOTT #   UNUSED CATALOGUE VALUE         PERCENT
 4                 1984      1985                 CHANGE
 5       -----------------------------------------------------------------
 6       Cxxx      50.00     100.00               @IF(B6<=0,0,(((C6-B6)/B6)*100))
 7       Cxxx                20.00                 @IF(B7<=0,0,(((C7-B7)/B7)*100))
 8
 9
10
11
12
13
14
15
16
17
18
19
20
```

We turned this formula display on by entering the command:

/Range,Format,Text,E6.E100↵

We also extended column E to 35 positions so we could see the entire formula on our screen by moving the active cell to any cell in column E and entering the command:

/Worksheet,Column-Width,Set,35↵

Once we turn off the formula display by entering the command:

/Range,Format,Fixed,2↵,E6.E100↵

and reset column E to 9 positions by moving the active cell to any cell in column E and entering the command:

/Worksheet,Column-Width,Set,9↵

our model would appear as follows:

```
E6:  (F2)  @IF(B6<=0,0,(((C6-B6)/B6)*100))                          READY

        A          B          C        D        E        F       G       H
 1                US AIRMAIL COLLECTION
 2
 3      SCOTT #  UNUSED CATALOGUE VALUE         PERCENT
 4                 1984       1985             CHANGE
 5      ---------------------------------------------------
 6      Cxxx       50.00     100.00            100.00
 7      Cxxx                  20.00              0.00
 8
 9
10
11
12
13
14
15
16
17
18
19
20
```

Although we only used two entries to illustrate how we can compute the percentage changes in the items in our collection, we could easily add additional stamps to our collection or track the percentage changes in catalogue values over a number of years.

While we have focused our attention upon stamp collecting in this chapter, the reader can easily employ the same concepts to collecting coins and other objects d'art.

9

Personal Information Recorder

Concept

The hectic pace of day to day living usually causes us to procrastinate and put off till tomorrow things we should do today. Unfortunately, tomorrow never arrives for many of us, especially when we need information we should have previously recorded. In this chaper, we will use 1-2-3 to prepare a personal inventory record template. After this template is created, we can use it to enter key items of personal information that our spouse, a relative or we personally might require in the event of an emergency or perhaps use simply to facilitate the recall of information as a requirement for that information occurs. Since the template presented in this chapter is quite comprehensive, it can also be used as a guide or checklist by the reader in considering items he or she may currently lack and which may be important, such as wills, trusts and other items.

Developing the Model

Since the primary purpose of this model is to facilitate the recording and updating of personal data, we will simply enter each major record category, permitting easy entry of the relevant data elements the reader may wish to record. Of course, since no two persons will have the same requirements, the reader is encouraged to use the following model as a guide for the development of his or her personal information record.

After entering a heading into cell C1 of our model, we can simply enter the headings for the information we require to be recorded into column A. A partial display of our model in figure 9.1 illustrates this concept. Note that at this point in time we have not changed the display format of 1-2-3 and are using its default width of 9 column positions. Here, the headings appear in full as entered since there is no data entered in column B that would normally block the display of data entered into column A that exceeds 9 character positions.

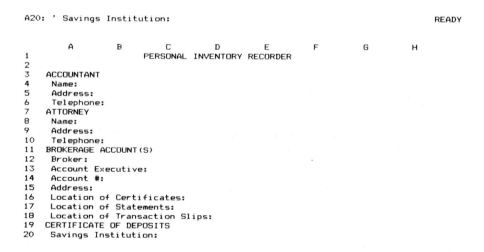

Figure 9.1. Personal Information Recorder headings (partial display)

In certain situations where we have multiple items that fall under one category heading, we may wish to change the format shown in figure 9.1. An example of this might be the credit card category which would appear as follows if we follow a single format in our model.

```
A37:                                                                    READY

          A       B          C          D          E        F        G        H
33   CREDIT CARDS
34    Issuer:
35    Card #:
36    Telephone # to report if lost:
37
38
39
40
41
42
43
44
45
46
47
48
49
50
51
52
```

If we are like many persons, we probably have multiple credit cards. If so, we could enter the headings for each card one by one down column A or we could reformat our headings as follows:

```
A36:                                                                    READY

          A       B          C          D          E        F        G        H
33   CREDIT CARDS
34    Issuer:                        Card #:   Telephone # to report if lost:
35
36
37
38
39
40
41
42
43
44
45
46
47
48
49
50
51
52
```

By reformatting the headings, we only have to enter the heading once and can then enter the data directly under each of the three columns.

To facilitate the construction of the Personal Information Recorder, we will list the contents of the headings entered into column A in table 9.1. Note that some text entries are preceded by one blank while a few are preceded by two blanks. These blanks were included in the headings to denote subcategories of data.

Table 9.1. Personal Information Recorder headings

```
A3:  'ACCOUNTANT
A4:  ' Name:
A5:  ' Address:
A6:  ' Telephone:
A7:  'ATTORNEY
A8:  ' Name:
A9:  ' Address:
A10: ' Telephone:
A11: 'BROKERAGE ACCOUNT(S)
A12: ' Broker:
A13: ' Account Executive:
A14: ' Account #:
A15: ' Address:
A16: ' Location of Certificates:
A17: ' Location of Statements:
A18: ' Location of Transaction Slips:
A19: 'CERTIFICATE OF DEPOSITS
A20: ' Savings Institution:
A21: ' Address:
A22: ' Principal AMOUNT:
A23: ' Interest rate:
A24: ' Maturity date:
A25: ' Account #:
A26: ' Location of certificates:
A27: 'CHECKING ACCOUNTS
A28: ' Name of Institution:
A29: ' Account #:
A30: ' Address:
A31: ' Location of checkbook:
A32: ' Where cancelled checks kept:
A33: 'CREDIT CARDS
A34: ' Issuer:
```

continued on following page

Table 9.1.(cont.) Personal Information Recorder headings

```
A35:  ' Card #:
A36:  ' Telephone # to report if lost:
A37:  'EMPLOYEE BENEFITS
A38:  ' Description:
A39:  ' Location of benefit statement:
A40:  ' Company contact:
A41:  'HOME MORTGAGE
A42:  ' Company:
A43:  ' Address:
A44:  ' Amount of monthly payments:
A45:  ' Payment due date in month:
A46:  ' Account #:
A47:  ' Where payment tickets kept:
A48:  'INSURANCE
A49:  ' AUTOMOBILE INSURANCE
A50:  '   Company:
A51:  '   Policy #:
A52:  '   Agent:
A53:  '   Where policy kept:
A54:  ' HOME INSURANCE
A55:  '   Company:
A56:  '   Policy #:
A57:  '   Agent:
A58:  '   Where policy kept:
A59:  ' LIFE INSURANCE
A60:  '   Company:
A61:  '   Policy #:
A62:  '   Agent:
A63:  '   Amount:
A64:  '   Beneficies:
A65:  'IRA ACCOUNT(S)
A66:  ' Company:
A67:  ' Address:
A68:  ' Account #:
A69:  ' Balance:
A70:  ' Location of statements:
A71:  'KEOGH ACCOUNT(S)
A72:  ' Company:
A73:  ' Address:
```

continued on following page

Table 9.1.(cont.)   Personal Information Recorder headings

```
A74:  ' Account #:
A75:  ' Balance:
A76:  ' Location of statements:
A77:  'KEYS
A78:  ' Automobile key code #:
A79:  ' Home key code #:
A80:  'MONEY MARKET ACCOUNTS
A81:  ' Company:
A82:  ' Address:
A83:  ' Account #:
A84:  ' Balance:
A85:  ' Location of statements:
A86:  'REAL ESTATE INVESTMENTS
A87:  ' Property address:
A88:  ' Mortgage company:
A89:  ' Account #:
A90:  ' Monthly payment:
A91:  ' Payment due date in month:
A92:  ' Location of payment tickets:
A93:  ' Where tax records kept:
A94:  'SAFE DEPOSIT BOX
A95:  ' Location:
A96:  ' Box number:
A97:  ' Where key(s) kept:
A98:  ' Where inventory kept:
A99:  'SAVINGS ACCOUNTS
A100:  ' Name of institution:
A101:  ' Address:
A102:  ' Account #:
A103:  ' Balance:
A104:  ' Location of savings book:
A105:  'SERIAL # OF ELECTRONIC EQUIPMENT
A106:  ' Computer:
A107:  ' Stereo:
A108:  ' TV set(s):
A109:  'TAX RECORDS
A110:  ' Location of records:
A111:  'TRUSTS
A112:  ' Type:
```

continued on following page

Table 9.1.(cont.)   Personal Information Recorder headings

```
A113:  ' Location of originals:
A114:  ' Location of copies:
A115:  'WILLS
A116:  ' Where original kept:
A117:  ' Where copies kept:
```

Once you have entered your headings into column A, you will probably want to reformat the model to facilitate the entry of the data items to be recorded. In examining the headings entered into column A, the longest entry was 31 character positions. This means that if we reformat column A to a width of 33 character positions, we can directly enter data into column B and always have at least one blank position between the heading in column A and the data entered into column B. To accomplish this, we would move the active cell to any cell in column A and enter the command:

/**W**orksheet,**C**olumn-Width,Set,33⁻⌐

Once column A is reformatted to a width of 33 positions, we can enter our data to be recorded into the appropriate row position of column B. After our entries are completed, we can print our model. Thus, a portion of our completed model might appear in printed form as follows:

```
ACCOUNTANT
  Name:                    Duwe Cheatum
  Address:                 5 Shylocka Court, Macon, GA 31210
  Telephone:               912-477-XXXX
```

Once our model is completed, we should save it as the personal possessions and financial circumstances of most persons vary with time. We can save our model by using the /**FS** command, entering:

/File,Save,**B:PRECORD**⁻⌐

to save our model on the diskette in drive B under the filename PRE-CORD. Now, we can easily retrieve the model at a later date by using the /**FR** command, modifying the entries to reflect changes in our personal situation.

Modifications to Consider

One can easily add or delete row entries by using the /**WIR** or /**WDR** commands to tailor the Personal Information Recorder to one's particular situation. One may also add a date to the model which should be prominently displayed when a printed report is generated. This would assist persons in determining that they are working with the latest version of the recorder since persons tend to print out this report either on a scheduled basis or randomly before business trips and give it to their spouse.

10

Forms Generator

Concept

Although there are obviously major differences between a word processor program and a spreadsheet program, one can use the capability of 1-2-3 to generate and print a variety of forms including form letters. The ability to use 1-2-3 in this manner is based upon 1-2-3's **F2** Function Key command that allows one to easily edit individual cell contents and the /**WCS** command that can be used to increase the width of a column to a full screen width of 80 character positions.

Constructing a Form

Suppose we wish to compose and distribute a letter to the parents of Troop #007, inviting them to attend the annual award banquet. Although this type of letter would normally be a candidiate for a word processing program, we could easily modify the cell format of 1-2-3 and use this spreadsheet to create and customize our form letter to each parent. By following the construction of the following model, the reader can use a similar approach for the construction of a variety of forms, ranging in scope from legal affidavits and bills of sale to a number of rental agreements. Once each form is entered and saved to a file, all one has to do is load the file and make the appropriate editing changes to customize the form to one's particular requirements.

To correspond to the number of print positions on one line of our form, we can set the width of column A to 60 character positions if we intend to print our form in noncompressed mode and to 120 character positions if we will print our form in a compressed print mode. Assuming the former, we would move the active cell to any cell in column A and enter the command:

/**W**orksheet,**C**olumn-Width,**S**et,**60** ⏎

Now that column A is set to a width of 60 character positions, we can enter our letter into the model on a row by row basis into cells A1, A2 and so on. As we enter the relevant information into the model on a row by row basis, we can use the 1-2-3 status line as a guide to when we should complete one cell entry and move the active cell to the next row. Since the status line shows the data as it is entered into the line, all one has to do is to examine the character position and terminate the entry on a word boundary as the character position of data being entered approaches, reaches or slightly exceeds the right side of the screen. Although this will not provide us with a right justified letter nor give us the word wrap capability of a word processor, it will nevertheless result in an effective form. Since we will not use column B in the model, if the data entered into column A exceeds the 60 character position width of that column the overflow will be displayed in a portion of column B.

As we enter the data into each row, we can use the 1-2-3 editing features to edit our entry or we can use the **F2** Function Key command to edit data previously entered into cells. Thus, we could use the left and right arrow keys to position the cursor to the desired location on the current line and then type insertions or use the delete key to make the desired modifications. Suppose our initial form letter was entered as follows:

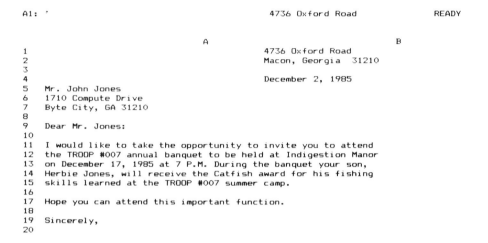

```
A1: '                                           4736 Oxford Road                    READY

                                      A                                     B
1                                          4736 Oxford Road
2                                          Macon, Georgia  31210
3
4                                          December 2, 1985
5     Mr. John Jones
6     1710 Compute Drive
7     Byte City, GA 31210
8
9     Dear Mr. Jones:
10
11    I would like to take the opportunity to invite you to attend
12    the TROOP #007 annual banquet to be held at Indigestion Manor
13    on December 17, 1985 at 7 P.M. During the banquet your son,
14    Herbie Jones, will receive the Catfish award for his fishing
15    skills learned at the TROOP #007 summer camp.
16
17    Hope you can attend this important function.
18
19    Sincerely,
20
```

Once our letter is entered, we could then save it to disk. Thus, entering the command:

/File,Save,B:FORM⏎

would save our form letter on the diskette in drive B under the filename FORM.

Now, suppose we wish to print the letter to Mr. Jones. Entering the command:

/Print,Printer,Range,A1.A23⏎**,Go,Page,Quit**

would cause our form letter to be printed as indicated in figure 10.1.

```
                                        4736 Oxford Road
                                        Macon, Georgia   31210

                                        December 2, 1985

Mr. John Jones
1710 Compute Drive
Byte City, GA 31210

Dear Mr. Jones:

I would like to take the opportunity to invite you to attend
the TROOP #007 annual banquet to be held at Indigestion Manor
on December 17, 1985 at 7 P.M. During the banquet your son,
Herbie Jones, will receive the Catfish award for his fishing
skills learned at the TROOP #007 summer camp.

Hope you can attend this important function.

Sincerely,


Gilbert Held
TROOP #007
```

Figure 10.1.   Printed form letter to Mr. Jones

Suppose we take a break from our tedious effort and return to our computer a few hours later desiring to send a similar letter to Mr. Williams. After loading 1-2-3, we would then load the form letter model by entering the command:

/File,Retrieve,B:FORM↵

Next, we could edit our model to make the relevant changes to our form. Thus, after a few lines of editing, our model might appear similar to figure 10.2.

Once our editing is completed, we could then print our new, personalized letter. We could then repeat this process for each of the parents in Troop #007, in effect, using 1-2-3 as a simple forms generator program.

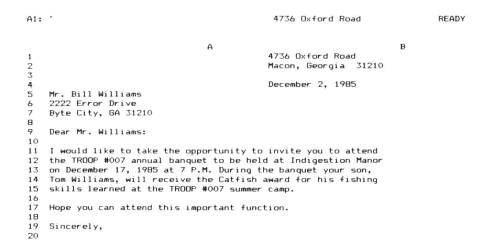

A1: '   4736 Oxford Road   READY

```
                                         A                          4736 Oxford Road                    B
1                                                                   4736 Oxford Road
2                                                                   Macon, Georgia   31210
3
4                                                                   December 2, 1985
5      Mr. Bill Williams
6      2222 Error Drive
7      Byte City, GA 31210
8
9      Dear Mr. Williams:
10
11     I would like to take the opportunity to invite you to attend
12     the TROOP #007 annual banquet to be held at Indigestion Manor
13     on December 17, 1985 at 7 P.M. During the banquet your son,
14     Tom Williams, will receive the Catfish award for his fishing
15     skills learned at the TROOP #007 summer camp.
16
17     Hope you can attend this important function.
18
19     Sincerely,
20
```

Figure 10.2. Form letter edited for Mr. Williams

11

Grade Recorder

Concept

Since many teachers grade student assignments, quizzes and examinations at home, a spreadsheet model to record grades can be used as a supplement or replacement for the traditional instructor's "blue book". In addition to recording grades, we can construct a model that can be used to compute midterm or final course grades based upon the weight we wish to assign to the various components of course work.

Constructing the Model

If the registrar does not provide us with a list of students in alphabetical order, we can use the **/DS** command to obtain a list of students structured in this manner.

97

Suppose we passed around the classroom a sheet of paper and asked each student to print his or her name on it. Then, at home we could create a column heading of "STUDENT" and enter the names of the students in the order they were written on the previously referenced paper.

Prior to entering the students' names, we should widen column A by using the /**WCS** command. If we believe 25 positions for the student name is sufficient, we would position the active cell to any cell in column A and enter the command:

/**W**orksheet,**C**olumn-Width,**S**et,**25**⏎

Our initial model with STUDENT centered in cell A1 and 10 student names entered in cells A3 through A12 in the order written onto the paper passed around the classroom might appear similar to figure 11.1.

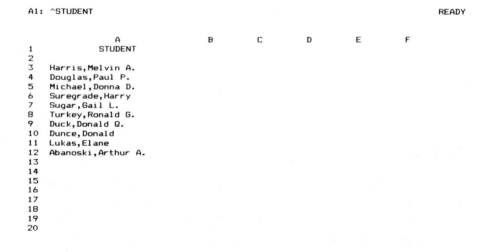

Figure 11.1. Initial student name entries

Since we might prefer to have our student list in alphabetical order, we could use the /**DS** command to resequence the student names entered into cells A3 through A12. Thus, we would enter:

/**D**ata,**S**ort,**D**ata-Range,**A3.A12**⏎,**P**rimary-Key,**A3**⏎,**A**⏎,**G**o

The preceding command would inform 1-2-3 that we want column A from rows 3 through 12 arranged in ascending sequence. After entering this command, our model would appear as in figure 11.2.

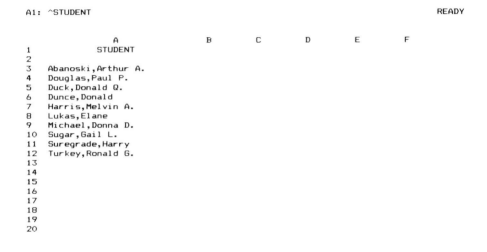

```
A1:   ^STUDENT                                                        READY

                  A             B        C        D        E        F
 1             STUDENT
 2
 3     Abanoski,Arthur A.
 4     Douglas,Paul P.
 5     Duck,Donald Q.
 6     Dunce,Donald
 7     Harris,Melvin A.
 8     Lukas,Elane
 9     Michael,Donna D.
10     Sugar,Gail L.
11     Suregrade,Harry
12     Turkey,Ronald G.
13
14
15
16
17
18
19
20
```

Figure 11.2.   Model after sorting student names

Now, let us continue the development of our grade recorder. Suppose we have preplanned our course activities to the point where we anticipate we will give one quiz and two homework assignments as well as a midterm examination. These four grading activities will form the basis for the midterm grade we will assign each student. We could enter the heading for each of these grading events into cell B1 through F1 as illustrated in figure 11.3.

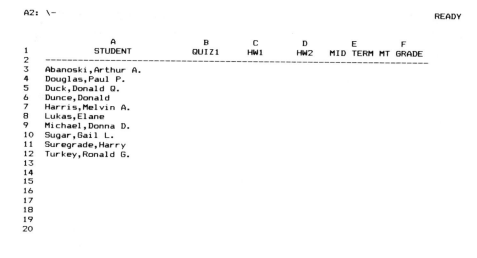

Figure 11.3. Model after addition of headings

Suppose the weight factors we wish to assign to each of the grading activities for the midterm grade are indicated in table 11.1.

Table 11.1. Midterm Weight Factors

Grading Event	Weight Factor
Quiz 1	10%
HW Assignment 1	20%
HW Assignment 2	30%
Midterm Examination	40%

Using the factors in table 11.1, it would be a time consuming task to compute the midterm grade by hand if there were more than a few students in our class. If we wish to construct a grade recorder, a little additional effort will permit us to automatically compute the midterm grade for each student once his or her grading events are entered into our model.

Based upon the weight factors contained in table 11.1, we would enter the formula (.1*B3+.2*C3+.3*D3+.4*E3) into cell F3. Then, we would use the /C command to copy this formula through cells F4 to F12. To do this we would enter the following command:

/Copy,F3⏎,F4.F12⏎

After the copy operation is completed, the contents of cells F3 through F12 will become:

```
F3:    (0.1*B3+0.2*C3+0.3*D3+0.4*E3)
F4:    (0.1*B4+0.2*C4+0.3*D4+0.4*E4)
F5:    (0.1*B5+0.2*C5+0.3*D5+0.4*E5)
F6:    (0.1*B6+0.2*C6+0.3*D6+0.4*E6)
F7:    (0.1*B7+0.2*C7+0.3*D7+0.4*E7)
F8:    (0.1*B8+0.2*C8+0.3*D8+0.4*E8)
F9:    (0.1*B9+0.2*C9+0.3*D9+0.4*E9)
F10:   (0.1*B10+0.2*C10+0.3*D10+0.4*E10)
F11:   (0.1*B11+0.2*C11+0.3*D11+0.4*E11)
F12:   (0.1*B12+0.2*C12+0.3*D12+0.4*E12)
```

Now, we are ready to enter student grades into our model after each grading activity. Once four grading activities for each student are entered the midterm grade will be computed automatically based upon the weight factors for each grading event established in table 11.1. Since we will probably enter each grading event at a different time, we will want to save our model and access it to enter student grades throughout the school year. To save our model, we can use the /FS command as follows:

/File,Save,B:STUDENT⏎

The preceding command would save our model on the diskette in drive B under the filename STUDENT.

Once we have entered four grades for each student, our model might appear as illustrated in figure 11.4.

A1: ^STUDENT   READY

```
                A              B       C       D       E       F
1            STUDENT         QUIZ1    HW1     HW2   MID TERM MT GRADE
2      -----------------------------------------------------------------
3      Abanoski,Arthur A.      75      83      92       97     90.5
4      Douglas,Paul P.         88      78      91       78     82.9
5      Duck,Donald Q.          72      76      80       67     73.2
6      Dunce,Donald            45      61      77       87     74.6
7      Harris,Melvin A.        86      70      67       70     70.7
8      Lukas,Elane             83      78      98       60     77.3
9      Michael,Donna D.        97      74      93       62     77.2
10     Sugar,Gail L.           76      70      67       74     71.3
11     Suregrade,Harry         66      90      88       77     81.8
12     Turkey,Ronald G.        45      80      86       70     74.3
13
14
15
16
17
18
19
20
```

Figure 11.4. Model after entering grades

Modifications to Consider

One of the questions we might ask is what happens if we have more than four grading events as this would force the display to scroll. For such cases, we could use the /**WTV** command to lock column A into place. Here, we would position the cursor into column B and enter the command:

/Worksheet,Titles,Vertical↵

The preceding command would lock column A into place. This would permit us to move the active cell to the right until column G were placed next to column A on our display. Then we could enter a grading event title into cell G1 and be able to easily enter the grades for each student as their names would be adjacent to this newly added grading event.

Suppose we wish to print just the names of the students and their midterm grade. Since the student name is contained in column A and the midterm grade is in column F, entering the range A1.F12 in a /**PPR** command would cause the data in columns B, C and D to be printed in addition to the data in columns A and B. Although this might not be a problem, if we add additional grading events we will reach a point where the student name and midterm or final grade columns are separated by too many event columns to be printed together across one line. For such situations, the /M command becomes significant. To see how we can use this command, let us assume we wish to print a list of students followed by their midterm grades. To do this, we must print the data in columns A and F next to each other. By entering:

/Move,B1.F12⤶,C1⤶
/Move,G1.G12⤶,B1⤶

column B through F are moved to the right one column, and column G, which was previously column F, is transferred to column B. Now we can produce a printed copy of student names and midterm grades by entering the command:

/Print,Printer,Range,A1.B12⤶,Go,Page,Quit

As a result of the preceding command, our midterm grade report would appear as follows:

STUDENT	MT GRADE
Abanoski,Arthur A.	90.5
Douglas,Paul P.	82.9
Duck,Donald Q.	73.2
Dunce,Donald	74.6
Harris,Melvin A.	70.7
Lukas,Elane	77.3
Michael,Donna D.	77.2
Sugar,Gail L.	71.3
Suregrade,Harry	81.8
Turkey,Ronald G.	74.3

The grade recorder model presented should be viewed as an illustration of how 1-2-3 can assist the teacher in the recording and computing of student grades. The weight assigned to the various events in our hypothetical course can be easily tailored to the grading structure one desires. In addition, one can easily add or eliminate classroom events and restructure the model for his or her particular course.

12

Homeowner Association Assessments

Concept

With Americans wanting more for their housing dollars, a large number of homeowner associations have been incorporated to maintain common community grounds and establish and maintain such properties as a community swimming pool, tennis courts, and other recreation facilities.

Typically, homeowner associations are funded by assessing each of their members a fee that may be based upon a percentage of the value of each member's property or could be a flat fee per home. One of the methods commonly employed to encourage members to pay their association dues on time is to restrict access to community recreation facilities to members in good financial standing.

In this chapter, we will first examine how we can use 1-2-3 to develop a model to assess association dues. After this model is completed, we will modify it to prepare a list of delinquent members that could be used by the association to restrict access to community recreation facilities to members in good standing.

The Dues Assessment Model

Since one does not require the use of a spreadsheet to compute member dues based upon a flat fee per home basis, we will first focus our attention on the situation where dues are based on a percentage of the value of each home. For simplicity of illustration, let us assume there are only 10 members in our association. Thus, our initial model would require 10 entries for the association member names, addresses and property values.

We can preplan the structure of our initial model by constructing a table of its data element values. Then, we can use the values in this table as a guide for entering our column headings as well as for setting the width and display format of each column. Let us assume that based upon an analysis of the members in our association, we developed table 12.1 that shows the data elements.

Table 12.1. Homeowner Association Data Elements

Column	Heading	Column Width	Format
A	Member	20	default
B	Property Address	17	default
C	Property Value	15	money display

Based upon the data elements in table 12.1, we must change the column width from the 1-2-3 default value of 9 to the numbers indicated in the table by using the /**WCS** command. Thus, we would move the active cell to any cell in column A and enter the command:

/**Worksheet,Column-Width,Set,20**↵

to change the width of column A to 20 positions. Similarly, we would enter 17 for the width in a second /**WCS** command and 15 in a third /**WCS** command to change the widths of columns B and C, remembering to move the active cell to the proper column before issuing the command.

Since we will be entering text data into columns A and B, we do not have to change the display format of these columns as text data will be left justified when entered into each cell which will normally be acceptable for our model. For the property value, we will most likely wish to display data as monetary values with 2 digits after the decimal point. Thus, we would use the /**RFF** command to set the display of the data in column C to a money format by entering the command:

/**R**ange,**F**ormat,**F**ixed,**2**-⌐,**C1.C14**-⌐

Now that we have set our column width and display format, let us enter a heading into our model and define an area into which we will enter the assessment percentage. After completion of these entries, we find that our model might appear as follows:

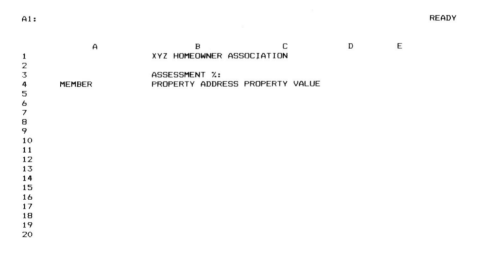

```
A1:                                                                READY


              A              B            C          D      E
 1                    XYZ HOMEOWNER ASSOCIATION
 2
 3                    ASSESSMENT %:
 4    MEMBER          PROPERTY ADDRESS PROPERTY VALUE
 5
 6
 7
 8
 9
10
11
12
13
14
15
16
17
18
19
20
```

Since the assessment percentage will be multiplied by the property value, to obtain the dues for each member we must add a column to contain these entries. Assuming we have decided to set the width of column D to 10 positions and use a money display format for this column, we would move the active cell to any cell in column D and enter the commands:

/Worksheet,Column-Width,Set,10↵

/Range,Format,Fixed,2↵,D1.D15↵

After entering the heading for this column in cell D4, we would then enter the formula @ROUND(C$3*C5,2) into cell D5 to compute the assessment of the first homeowner based upon his or her property value rounded to 2 decimal places. Here, we are multiplying the assessment percentage that will be entered into cell C3 by the homeowner's property value to compute the association dues. Since we will enter the data for 10 members into our model, we must copy this formula through cell D14. This is accomplished by using the /C command as follows:

/Copy,D5↵,D6.D14↵

Since the assessment percentage remains constant, we would enter the reference to cell C3 in the formula as C$3, which indicates to 1-2-3 that this is an absolute cell reference. This results in the /Copy command always leaving the copied formulas referencing the absolute cell C3. Once the copy process is completed, the contents of cells D4 through D14 to include our column heading are as as follows:

```
D4:   (F2)   'ASSESSMENT
D5:   (F2)   @ROUND(C$3*C5,2)
D6:   (F2)   @ROUND(C$3*C6,2)
D7:   (F2)   @ROUND(C$3*C7,2)
D8:   (F2)   @ROUND(C$3*C8,2)
D9:   (F2)   @ROUND(C$3*C9,2)
D10:  (F2)   @ROUND(C$3*C10,2)
D11:  (F2)   @ROUND(C$3*C11,2)
D12:  (F2)   @ROUND(C$3*C12,2)
D13:  (F2)   @ROUND(C$3*C13,2)
D14:  (F2)   @ROUND(C$3*C14,2)
```

Let us assume that our homeowner budget for next year is antici-pated to be $8,450 and we wish to determine the percentage of property value to use our assessment. To accomplish this task, we would enter the data for each homeowner into our model and then enter the formula @SUM(D5.D14) into cell D15 and label TOTAL: into cell C15. Our model might appear similar to figure 12.1.

```
A1:                                                             READY


            A                    B              C         D        E
1                          XYZ HOMEOWNER ASSOCIATION
2
3                          ASSESSMENT %:
4        MEMBER            PROPERTY ADDRESS PROPERTY VALUE ASSESSMENT
5    Mr. Donald Arron      4712 Fairway Dr.      47500.00      0.00
6    Mr. Herbert Baker     4714 Fairway Dr.      49775.00      0.00
7    Ms. Donna Duck        4716 Fairway Dr.      43750.00      0.00
8    Mr/Mrs Rubin Elf      4720 Fairway Dr.      48400.00      0.00
9    Ms. Elaine Gelda      62 Beachway Dr.       74500.00      0.00
10   Mr/Mrs Harry Harp     68 Beachway Dr.       77750.00      0.00
11   Mr/Mrs Stanley Ida    70 Beachway Dr.       82500.00      0.00
12   Mr. Mike Jones        10 Parkway Pl.        42500.00      0.00
13   Ms. Morgan Memmel     14 Parkway Pl.        44750.00      0.00
14   Mr/Mrs Seymore Glic   20 Parkway Pl.        43250.00      0.00
15                                      TOTAL:                 0.00
16
17
18
19
20
```

Figure 12.1. Model after entry of homeowner data

If our first guess entered into cell C3 has more than 2 decimal digits, we will note that only the first 2 digits are displayed, although 1-2-3 accepts a maximum of 16 decimal places for a numeric constant. Since we previously set column C to display data with 2 decimal digits, we must set the display format of cell C3 to number of digits we desire to be displayed in that cell. Assuming 6 decimal digits will satisfy our requirement, we will first enter the command:

/Range,Format,Fixed,6↵,C3↵

which would cause cell C3 to display data with 6 decimal positions.

Now, through a trial and error process, we can determine the assess-ment percentage required to obtain the $8,250 budget for our association.

If we enter .03 percent into cell C3, cell D15 will indicate a total assessment of $16,640.25. Since this amount is greater than our budget requirement, we would then enter a smaller assessment percentage into cell C3 and 1-2-3 will automatically recompute the individual and total assessments. After a number of trial and error iterations, entering .014875 percent would result in a total assessment of $8,250.79, which might be sufficiently accurate for our association and our model would appear as follows:

```
C3: (F6) 0.014875                                                    READY

               A              B            C          D        E
 1                     XYZ HOMEOWNER ASSOCIATION
 2
 3                     ASSESSMENT %:          0.014875
 4     MEMBER          PROPERTY ADDRESS PROPERTY VALUE ASSESSMENT
 5     Mr. Donald Arron     4712 Fairway Dr.    47500.00    706.56
 6     Mr. Herbert Baker    4714 Fairway Dr.    49775.00    740.40
 7     Ms. Donna Duck       4716 Fairway Dr.    43750.00    650.78
 8     Mr/Mrs Rubin Elf     4720 Fairway Dr.    48400.00    719.95
 9     Ms. Elaine Gelda     62 Beachway Dr.     74500.00   1108.19
10     Mr/Mrs Harry Harp    68 Beachway Dr.     77750.00   1156.53
11     Mr/Mrs Stanley Ida   70 Beachway Dr.     82500.00   1227.19
12     Mr. Mike Jones       10 Parkway Pl.      42500.00    632.19
13     Ms. Morgan Memmel    14 Parkway Pl.      44750.00    665.66
14     Mr/Mrs Seymore Glic  20 Parkway Pl.      43250.00    643.34
15                                TOTAL:                   8250.79
16
17
18
19
20
```

Figure 12.2. Total assessment of association model

We could eliminate the trial and error approach to computing the assessment percentage by summing the property values and dividing the sum into the association budget. We could place the assessment percentage computation in any free location in the spreadsheet. Thus, if we use cell C16 to hold the assessment percentage computation, we would enter the formula 8250/@SUM(C5.C14) into cell C16, alleviating the previously described trial and error process. Obviously, we would then have to modify the formulas previously entered into cell D5 through D14. Thus, the entry in cell D5 would become @ROUND(C$16*C5,2) and so on.

MODIFYING THE MODEL

Let us assume our association bills members on an annual basis and we wish to record the payment status of each member. We can add a PAYMENT column to our model in column E. Since we will normally want the data in this column displayed in a money format with 2 digits after the decimal point, we would enter the command:

/Range,Format,Fixed,2-⌐,E1.E20-⌐

Let us also assume that association bills were mailed 30 days ago and we have updated our model to include a column denoting the payments received. If we wish to obtain a printout of our model at this point, we are probably approaching the 80 character per row limit of most printers and thus may desire to place our printer into its compressed printing mode. Assuming we have an EPSON MX-80 printer, this can be accomplished by entering the command:

/Print,Printer,Options,Setup,\015-⌐,Quit,Quit

with the \015 indicating to 1-2-3 that we wish to change the default printing specifications to compressed print mode. To print the desired range of our model, we would use the command:

/Print,Printer,Range,A1.E15-⌐,Go,Page,Quit

Thus, our model would then appear printed as illustrated in figure 12.3.

If we wish to use this model to generate a list of the status of association members, we can add another column to the model and label it with the heading STATUS. After entering STATUS into cell F4, we will then enter the formula @IF(E5>=D5,@NA,@ERR) into cell F5. As a result of this formula, the textual constant NA will be entered into cell F5 if the contents of cell E5 (payment) are greater than or equal to the contents of cell D5 (assessment) while the textual constant ERR would be entered if one did not pay or did not pay in full his or her assessment. Once the preceding formula is entered into cell F5, we will then copy it through cell F6 to F14, using the /C command. After this copy command is executed, our model will appear as shown in figure 12.4.

XYZ HOMEOWNER ASSOCIATION

MEMBER	PROPERTY ADDRESS	PROPERTY VALUE	ASSESSMENT	PAYMENT
	ASSESSMENT %:	0.014875		
Mr. Donald Arron	4712 Fairway Dr.	47500.00	706.56	706.56
Mr. Herbert Baker	4714 Fairway Dr.	49775.00	740.40	0.00
Ms. Donna Duck	4716 Fairway Dr.	43750.00	650.78	650.78
Mr/Mrs Rubin Elf	4720 Fairway Dr.	48400.00	719.95	719.95
Ms. Elaine Gelda	62 Beachway Dr.	74500.00	1108.19	1108.19
Mr/Mrs Harry Harp	68 Beachway Dr.	77750.00	1156.53	500.00
Mr/Mrs Stanley Ida	70 Beachway Dr.	82500.00	1227.19	1227.19
Mr. Mike Jones	10 Parkway Pl.	42500.00	632.19	632.19
Ms. Morgan Memmel	14 Parkway Pl.	44750.00	665.66	0.00
Mr/Mrs Seymore Glic	20 Parkway Pl.	43250.00	643.34	643.34
		TOTAL:	8250.79	

Figure 12.3. Printed homeowners association model

F5: @IF(E5>=D5,@NA,@ERR)   READY

	B	C	D	E	F	G
1	XYZ HOMEOWNER ASSOCIATION					
2						
3	ASSESSMENT %:	0.014875				
4	PROPERTY ADDRESS	PROPERTY VALUE	ASSESSMENT	PAYMENT	STATUS	
5	4712 Fairway Dr.	47500.00	706.56	706.56	NA	
6	4714 Fairway Dr.	49775.00	740.40	0.00	ERR	
7	4716 Fairway Dr.	43750.00	650.78	650.78	NA	
8	4720 Fairway Dr.	48400.00	719.95	719.95	NA	
9	62 Beachway Dr.	74500.00	1108.19	1108.19	NA	
10	68 Beachway Dr.	77750.00	1156.53	500.00	ERR	
11	70 Beachway Dr.	82500.00	1227.19	1227.19	NA	
12	10 Parkway Pl.	42500.00	632.19	632.19	NA	
13	14 Parkway Pl.	44750.00	665.66	0.00	ERR	
14	20 Parkway Pl.	43250.00	643.34	643.34	NA	
15		TOTAL:	8250.79			
16						
17						
18						
19						
20						

Figure 12.4. Model after status calculation

Suppose we wish to give the pool lifeguard a list of members and their status. Since their property values and assessments are normally considered confidential information, we may only want to furnish the lifeguard with the information contained in columns A and F, the member names and their payment status.

Since 1-2-3 only permits us to print the contents of a single cell or contiguous range of cells, we must first position columns A and F next to one another prior to using the /**PPR** command to make a hard copy of a recreation facility usage report. 1-2-3 contains both a move and a copy command that can be used to reformat a portion of our model to obtain the printed report we desire. If we used the move command to move the data in column F into column B, we would first have to copy the contents of column B into an empty column to avoid overwriting and losing it. Then, after our report is printed we would move the contents of column B back into column F and contents of the old column B from its new location back into column B.

If we will use the homeowner model on a periodic basis, it may be far easier to update and save that model and then simply move column F into column B to print the report we desire. Thus, we could save our assessment model by entering the command:

/File.Save,**B:HOMEDUES**↵

which would save our model under the filename HOMEDUES on the diskette in drive B. Now, we can manipulate our model to produce the recreation facility usage report without worrying about reconstructing our model back into its original format. To move the data in column F into column B, we would enter the command:

/**M**ove,**F1.F14**↵,**B1.B14**↵

To make column B more readable, we would reset the column width to 7 positions by moving the active cell to any cell in column B and entering the command:

/**W**orksheet,**C**olumn-Width,**S**et,**7**↵

Before we print our model, we must remember that we turned compressed print mode on during an earlier printing, and we must now be sure and turn compressed mode off. We can instruct 1-2-3 to turn compressed print mode off and print the model with following command:

/Print,Printer,Range,**A1.B14**⌐,Options,Setup,**(Esc)**⌐,Quit,Go,Page,Quit

Note that the (Esc) in the above command means to press the key marked "Esc" on the keyboard. This will remove the setup string which caused compressed print from the print command. Our report will appear in printed form as shown below.

MEMBER	STATUS
Mr. Donald Arron	NA
Mr. Herbert Baker	ERR
Ms. Donna Duck	NA
Mr/Mrs Rubin Elf	NA
Ms. Elaine Gelda	NA
Mr/Mrs Harry Harp	ERR
Mr/Mrs Stanley Ida	NA
Mr. Mike Jones	NA
Ms. Morgan Memmel	ERR
Mr/Mrs Seymore Glic	NA

It should be noted that we could easily add a heading into cell A2 prior to printing the report to indicate both the nature and date of the report.

Although we have developed and modified the homeowner association model in this report using only 10 members, we could easily have had 100, 200 or more members. As you can see, 1-2-3 is a very powerful analysis and report generating tool that is only limited by our imagination.

13

Life Insurance Analysis

Concept

Although most companies provide life insurance coverage to their personnel, it is the rare company that provides consulting assistance to help the employee determine if his or her total life insurance is sufficient or perhaps more than the employee needs. To assist the reader in determining an appropriate level of life insurance, we will develop a model that will calculate what your family would actually require if you should, unfortunately, die today. In addition, this model can be periodically updated to reflect changes in one's financial status and standard of living since insurance requirements can vary significantly during the course of your life. Since there are numerous variables that must be considered as well as the type of life insurance that will best fit one's financial circumstances, the reader may wish to discuss his or her financial situation with a financial planner or a life insurance agent.

The Life Insurance Analysis Model

In developing our model, we will first identify the funds necessary to be paid at one's death to include funeral expenses, estate taxes, attorney fees, bills and credit balances due. Next, we will consider a contingency fund that could include several months take-home pay if we do not have adequate savings to tide our family over and allow them to pay their living expenses, minor repairs and other day-to-day expenses we are all too familiar with.

Based upon the preceding, we can develop our model to permit us to enter the appropriate values for each of the expenses previously discussed into a column of cells in our spreadsheet. Thus, our initial model might appear as follows after we have entered our headings and the command:

/Worksheet,Global,Format,Text

to display formulas as they are entered.

```
D9:  @SUM(D4..D8)                                              READY

         A         B         C         D         E      F      G      H
 1                LIFE  INSURANCE  REQUIREMENT  ANALYSIS
 2
 3    IMMEDIATE EXPENSES
 4      FUNERAL:
 5      ESTATE TAXES:
 6      BILLS:
 7      CREDIT BALANCES:
 8      CONTINGENCY:
 9    TOTAL IMMEDIATE EXPENSES:    @SUM(D4.
10
11
12
13
14
15
16
17
18
19
20
```

Since we entered our expense estimates in column D, we entered the formula @SUM(D4.D8) into cell D9 to obtain a total of immediate expenses. Notice that we cannot see the entire formula in cell D4. This is because the default width of the column is 9 positions. We can change the width of column D to 17 positions by moving the active cell to any cell in column D and entering the /**WCS** command as follows:

/**W**orksheet,**C**olumn-Width,**S**et,**17**↵

Our worksheet now appears as follows:

```
D9:  @SUM(D4..D8)                                                    READY

         A        B        C        D        E        F        G
 1                LIFE INSURANCE REQUIREMENT ANALYSIS
 2
 3   IMMEDIATE EXPENSES
 4     FUNERAL:
 5     ESTATE TAXES:
 6     BILLS:
 7     CREDIT BALANCES:
 8     CONTINGENCY:
 9   TOTAL IMMEDIATE EXPENSES:    @SUM(D4..D8)
10
11
12
13
14
15
16
17
18
19
20
```

Now let us consider the expected living expenses of our family. Included in this category of expenses are such items as rent or mortgage payment, utility payments, automobile payments, insurance payments, clothing and food purchases as well as other day-to-day living expenses. If we wish, instead of estimating these expenses on an annual basis we can enter them as a more familiar monthly expense into one column and then multiply by 12 to obtain their yearly equivalent in another column. Thus, we could continue developing our model as follows:

```
D19: @SUM(D11..D18)                                              READY

         A          B         C           D              E      F      G
 1                    LIFE INSURANCE REQUIREMENT ANALYSIS
 2
 3   IMMEDIATE EXPENSES
 4    FUNERAL:
 5    ESTATE TAXES:
 6    BILLS:
 7    CREDIT BALANCES:
 8    CONTINGENCY:
 9   TOTAL IMMEDIATE EXPENSES:    @SUM(D4..D8)
10   LIVING EXPENSES    MONTHLY   ANNUAL
11    RENT/MORTGAGE:              +C11*12
12    UTILITIES:                  +C12*12
13    AUTOMOBILE:                 +C13*12
14    INSURANCE:                  +C14*12
15    CLOTHING:                   +C15*12
16    FOOD:                       +C16*12
17    VACATION:                   +C17*12
18    OTHER:                      +C18*12
19   TOTAL LIVING EXPENSES:       @SUM(D11..D18)
20
                                                                 CAPS
```

Since we will enter our monthly living expenses into column C from rows
11 through 18, we must multiply those entries by 12 to obtain their annual
equivalent in column D. Thus, we would enter the formula +C11*12 into
cell D11. Next, we could copy this formula through cell D18 by entering
the command:

/Copy,D11↵,D12.D18↵

To obtain the total living expenses on a monthly and annual basis, we
will now enter the formula @SUM(D11.D18) into cell D19.

If our wife works or our family is eligible for Social Security benefits
or a pension from our company, we may wish to consider such income as
an offset to the total living expenses of our family. Thus, we would add
the following items to our model:

```
D26:  +D19-D25                                                    READY

            A          B        C            D          E       F       G
   20  FAMILY INCOME
   21     PENSION:                        +C21*12
   22     SOCIAL SEC:                     +C22*12
   23     SPOUSE:                         +C23*12
   24     OTHER:                          +C24*12
   25  TOTAL FAMILY INCOME:               @SUM(D21..D24)
   26  NET LIVING EXPENSES:               +D19-D25
   27
   28
   29
   30
   31
   32
   33
   34
   35
   36
   37
   38
   39
                                                                  CAPS
```

Similar to the manner in which we handled living expenses, we can enter the data elements of family income in terms of the income received on a monthly basis into column C and multiply each entry by 12 to obtain the required annual amount in column D. We would enter the formula @SUM(D21.D24) into cell D25 to obtain the total family income on an annual basis. Since the net living expenses are the total living expenses less the total family income we would enter the formula +D19-D25 into cell D26.

Now that we know our family's net living expense requirement, we should project this amount over the number of years of the life expectancy of our spouse. Thus, we could add the following to our model.

```
D29:  +D26*D28                                                   READY

            A          B        C            D          E       F       G
   26  NET LIVING EXPENSES:               +D19-D25
   27  EXPECTED LIVING EXPENSES:
   28    YEARS TILL WIFE AGE XX:
   29  TOTAL LIVING EXPENSES:             +D26*D28
   30
   31
   32
   33
   34
   35
   36
   37
   38
   39
   40
   41
   42
   43
   44
   45
                                                                  CAPS
```

In the preceding additions to our model, we will enter the number of years until our spouse reaches his or her conservative life expectancy into cell D28 and then compute the total living expenses by multiplying that entry by the contents of cell D26. Thus, we would enter the formula +D26*D28 into cell D29.

If we have children and expect that they will go to college, we should account for this in our model as well as for any gifts to charities or organizations we might include in our will. Thus, we could add the following to our model:

```
D33: @SUM(D31..D32)                                          READY


          A         B          C          D          E      F      G
30   ONE TIME EXPENSES
31     COLLEGE FUND:
32     OTHER:
33   TOTAL ONE TIME:               @SUM(D31..D32)
34                        .
35
36
37
38
39
40
41
42
43
44
45
46
47
48
49
                                                              CAPS
```

If we enter our one-time expenses into column D, we would enter the formula @SUM(D31.D32) into cell D33.

Although we could simply add up the total immediate, living and one-time expenses and subtract our savings from this total, this procedure would not provide us with an accurate measurement of our life insurance needs. Since our insurance payment can be invested and earn interest, we should determine the present value of our spouse's living expenses. To accomplish this, we will use the 1-2-3 @PV function. Thus, we would add the following to our model:

```
D40: +D38-D39                                              READY

        A       B       C           D           E     F     G
34  INSURANCE REQUIREMENTS
35    LIVING EXPENSES:          @PV(D26,0.1,D28)
36    IMMEDIATE EXPENSES:       +D9
37    ONE TIME EXPENSES:        +D33
38  SUBTOTAL                    @SUM(D35..D37)
39  INVESTMENTS/SAVINGS:
40  LIFE INSURANCE NEEDS:       +D38-D39
41
42
43
44
45
46
47
48
49
50
51
52
53
                                                          CAPS
```

If we assume our spouse will be able to earn 10 percent interest on the insurance payment, we would enter the formula @PV(D26,.1,D28) into cell D35. Here, D26 represents the annual family living expenses, .1 represents 10 percent interest and D28 is the number of years our spouse requires living expenses.

Next we will add the insurance required to pay our immediate expenses and one-time expenses and then subtract the value of our investments from this total to determine our life insurance needs which basically completes our model.

Prior to exercising the model, we should consider our financial circumstances which may require us to change the default width of columns C and D from 9 positions to a larger number. In addition, we may wish to display our entries in those columns in a money display format. Thus, we could move the active cell to the appropriate column and enter the commands:

/Worksheet,Column-Width,Set,12↵
/Range,Format,Comma,2↵,C1.D40↵

to both set the width of columns C and D to 12 positions and display data in those columns in a money format with 2 decimal digits and commas.

Prior to entering some obviously fictitious data, let us save our model. Thus, we could enter the command:

/File,Save,B:LIFE⏎

if we wish to save our model under the filename LIFE on the diskette in drive B.

Figure 13.2 illustrates a completed model after we have printed it using the command:

/Print,Printer,Range,A1.D40⏎**,Go,Page,Quit**

```
        LIFE  INSURANCE  REQUIREMENT  ANALYSIS

IMMEDIATE EXPENSES
 FUNERAL:                               5,000.00
 ESTATE TAXES:                          2,000.00
 BILLS:                                 2,100.00
 CREDIT BALANCES:                         400.00
 CONTINGENCY:
TOTAL IMMEDIATE EXPENSES:               9,500.00
LIVING EXPENSES     MONTHLY       ANNUAL
 RENT/MORTGAGE:        750.00        9,000.00
 UTILITIES:            300.00        3,600.00
 AUTOMOBILE:           175.00        2,100.00
 INSURANCE:            125.00        1,500.00
 CLOTHING:             150.00        1,800.00
 FOOD:                 400.00        4,800.00
 VACATION:             100.00        1,200.00
 OTHER:                325.00        3,900.00
TOTAL LIVING EXPENSES:              27,900.00
FAMILY INCOME
 PENSION:              750.00        9,000.00
 SOCIAL SEC:           500.00        6,000.00
 SPOUSE:               100.00        1,200.00
 OTHER:                250.00        3,000.00
TOTAL FAMILY INCOME:               19,200.00
NET LIVING EXPENSES:                8,700.00
EXPECTED LIVING EXPENSES:
 YEARS TILL WIFE AGE XX:                25.00
TOTAL LIVING EXPENSES:            217,500.00
ONE TIME EXPENSES
 COLLEGE FUND:                      36,000.00
 OTHER:
TOTAL ONE TIME:                     36,000.00
INSURANCE REQUIREMENTS
 LIVING EXPENSES:                   78,970.25
 IMMEDIATE EXPENSES:                 9,500.00
 ONE TIME EXPENSES:                 36,000.00
SUBTOTAL                           124,470.25
INVESTMENTS/SAVINGS:
LIFE INSURANCE NEEDS:              124,470.25
```

Figure 13.3.   Completed Life Insurance Analysis model

14

Retirement Funding Analysis

Concept

Between January and April of each year, it is difficult to turn on a radio or read a newspaper without being exposed to advertisements concerning Individual Retirement Accounts (IRA) and Keogh Accounts. Based upon the ability to deduct one's contribution into these retirement plans to reduce federal tax liability, millions of persons haved opened accounts at banks, savings and loan institutions and brokerage companies. Since the earnings from interest or other investment gains contained in these accounts are tax deferred, one's retirement account can rapidly escalate in value. This is due to the fact that both the principal and earnings credited to the account remain in the account. In comparison, earnings from interest or other investment gains in conventional accounts may require one to withdraw a portion of the proceeds in the account to pay the tax liability due on such earnings each year.

For investors opening IRA or Keogh accounts, there are three particular areas of concern with respect to one's investment. First, one may have a goal concerning the sum he or she wishes to have available upon retirement and thus needs to determine the payments into the account that are required to accumulate this sum. Secondly, even if one has no fixed goal concerning the accumulation of a specific sum for retirement, one may still desire to project his or her retirement funds value based upon making fixed deposits into the fund over a period of time. Finally, if one establishes a retirement fund and prior to retirement requires the use of a portion of the fund, under current tax law he or she is subject to a 10 percent penalty. While this penalty serves as a deterrent to withdrawing funds prior to retirement, under certain situations the investor is financially better off to establish a retirement fund and withdraw the proceeds prior to retirement than if he or she had not established this fund. In our analysis, we will investigate the parameters that determine the length of one's investment and rate of interest that permit the investor to gain from establishing a retirement fund and withdrawing the proceeds prior to maturity in comparison to not establishing this type of fund.

In this chapter, we will develop three retirement models that can be used by the reader to analyze his or her retirement fund. Each of these models can be used as a separate entity, to analyze specific areas concerning retirement funds that may be relevant to the reader.

The Contribution Model

If we know the amount we wish our retirement account to contain at a certain period of time in the future, we can calculate the annual contributions required to obtain the fund value we desire at retirement. Furthermore, we can determine the annual report contributions based upon making our deposits at the beginning of the year, the annual contribution can be obtained by solving the following formula:

$$\text{Annual Contribution} = \frac{\text{Amount at Retirement}}{\sum\limits_{i=1}^{\text{Years}} \left(1+\dfrac{I}{m}\right)^{i*m}}$$

where:

Amount at Retirement	=	the amount we want in our retirement fund
Years	=	the number of years to retirement
m	=	the number of compounding periods per year interest is credited to our account
I	=	annual rate of interest/100

If the deposit is made at the end of the year, the annual contribution necessary to obtain the desired retirement sum is obtained by solving the following formula:

$$\text{Annual Contribution} = \frac{\text{Amount at Retirement}}{\sum\limits_{i=1}^{\text{Years}} \left(1+\dfrac{I}{m}\right)^{k*m}}$$

where: $k = i-1$

Suppose we want to determine the annual contributions necessary over a 20-year period to obtain a predefined sum for retirement. After we enter our headings into the model we can reserve a cell to contain the amount we desire at retirement and replicate the denominator of each formula through 20 cells to obtain the required iterations for the summation of the formula through 20 periods. Then we could use the 1-2-3 @SUM function to sum the denominators and divide that sum into the amount we wish to obtain at retirement, yielding our annual contribution.

Based upon the preceding, let us construct our contribution model. We can enter the headings into our model as shown in figure 14.1.

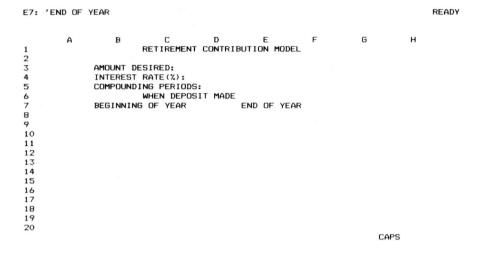

Figure 14.1. Contribution model headings

Note that we will enter the amount we wish to obtain at retirement, the anticipated interest rate our investment will earn and the number of compounding periods per year into cells D3 through D5.

Since the denominator is raised to the power i*m where i will vary from 1 to 20, we must obtain a mechanism to increment the value of i when we enter and replicate our formulas. We can easily accomplish this task by including a table of numbers varying from 1 to 20 in column A. This can be accomplished by entering 1 into cell A8 and the formula +A8+1 into cell A9. Then we would use the /C command to copy this formula through cell A27. Thus, we would enter the command:

/Copy,A9↵,A10.A27↵

Resulting in a table of values from 1 to 20 being established in cells A8 through A27.

Now we would enter the formula $(1+D\$4/D\$5)^{\wedge}(A8*D\$5)$ into cell C8 which is the denominator of the formula to determine the annual contributions if a deposit is made at the beginning of the year. Next we will copy this formula from cell C8 into cells C9 through C27 by entering the command:

/Copy,**C8**⏎,**C9.C27**⏎

Since the interest rate and number of compounding periods remain constant, we have placed absolute references to the cells D4 and D5 in the formula. In cell C28, we would enter the formula @SUM(C8.C27) while we would enter the formula +D3/C28 into cell C29 to obtain the annual contribution required if deposits are made at the beginning of the year. If we enter the command:

/**W**orksheet,**G**lobal,**F**ormat,**T**ext

our model at this time would appear as shown in figure 14.2.

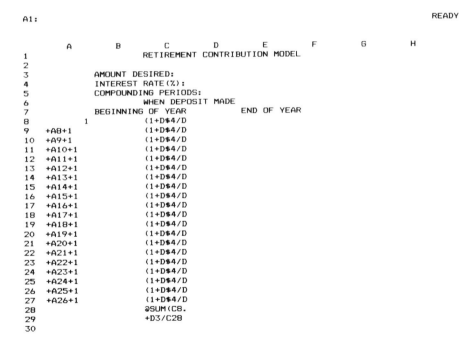

Figure 14.2. Contribution Model after formula entries

Notice that we cannot see the entire formula as the width of column C is only 9 positions. We can easily extend the width of column C to 26 positions by moving the active cell to any cell in column C and using the command:

/Worksheet,Column-Width,Set,26↵

Our model would appear as follows:

```
A1:                                                                    READY

          A         B                  C                 D       E        F
1                             RETIREMENT CONTRIBUTION MODEL
2
3                   AMOUNT DESIRED:
4                   INTEREST RATE(%):
5                   COMPOUNDING PERIODS:
6                         WHEN DEPOSIT MADE
7                   BEGINNING OF YEAR                         END OF YEAR
8                 1         (1+D$4/D$5)^(A8*D$5)
9         +A8+1           (1+D$4/D$5)^(A9*D$5)
10        +A9+1           (1+D$4/D$5)^(A10*D$5)
11        +A10+1          (1+D$4/D$5)^(A11*D$5)
12        +A11+1          (1+D$4/D$5)^(A12*D$5)
13        +A12+1          (1+D$4/D$5)^(A13*D$5)
14        +A13+1          (1+D$4/D$5)^(A14*D$5)
15        +A14+1          (1+D$4/D$5)^(A15*D$5)
16        +A15+1          (1+D$4/D$5)^(A16*D$5)
17        +A16+1          (1+D$4/D$5)^(A17*D$5)
18        +A17+1          (1+D$4/D$5)^(A18*D$5)
19        +A18+1          (1+D$4/D$5)^(A19*D$5)
20        +A19+1          (1+D$4/D$5)^(A20*D$5)
21        +A20+1          (1+D$4/D$5)^(A21*D$5)
22        +A21+1          (1+D$4/D$5)^(A22*D$5)
23        +A22+1          (1+D$4/D$5)^(A23*D$5)
24        +A23+1          (1+D$4/D$5)^(A24*D$5)
25        +A24+1          (1+D$4/D$5)^(A25*D$5)
26        +A25+1          (1+D$4/D$5)^(A26*D$5)
27        +A26+1          (1+D$4/D$5)^(A27*D$5)
28                        @SUM(C8..C27)
29                        +D3/C28
30
```

Similarly, we would enter the formula $(1+D\$4/D\$5)^{((A8-1)*D\$5)}$ into cell E8 and copy this formula into cells E9 through E27. Then we would enter the formula @SUM(E8.E27) into cell D28 and the formula +D3/D28 into cell D29 to obtain the annual contribution required if deposits are made at the end of the year. Then we could change column C back to 9 positions by moving the active cell to any cell in column C and entering the command:

/Worksheet,Column-Width,Set,9↵

Prior to exercising our model, we could modify it slightly to display the beginning and end of year contributions at the top portion of the model so we do not have to scroll to row 29 to see the results. Thus, we would enter the heading CONTRIBUTION REQUIRED into cell F3 and the headings BEGINNING and ' END into cells F4 and G4. Then, we would enter +C29 into cell F5 and +D29 into cell G5.

Now let us exercise our model. Turn the formulas display off with the command:

/Worksheet,Global,Format,General

Suppose we wish to obtain $50,000 at retirement and believe we can earn 14½% interest compounded quarterly during the life of our fund. We would enter 50000 into cell D3 and .145 into cell D4 and 4 into cell D5, resulting in the following display occurring on the first five lines of our model:

```
A1:                                                           READY

          A       B        C        D       E      F       G      H
    1                     RETIREMENT CONTRIBUTION MODEL
    2
    3             AMOUNT DESIRED:      50000         CONTRIBUTION REQUIRED
    4             INTEREST RATE(%):    0.145         BEGINNING   END
    5             COMPOUNDING PERIOD     4           408.1031 470.5742
    6                    WHEN DEPOSIT MADE
    7             BEGINNING OF YEAR          END OF YEAR
    8          1          1.153076              1
    9          2          1.329585          1.153076
   10          3          1.533114          1.329585
   11          4          1.767798          1.533114
   12          5          2.038406          1.767798
   13          6          2.350439          2.038406
   14          7          2.710236          2.350439
   15          8          3.125110          2.710236
   16          9          3.603492          3.125110
   17         10          4.155102          3.603492
   18         11          4.791151          4.155102
   19         12          5.524565          4.791151
   20         13          6.370246          5.524565
```

From the preceding, we would have to contribute $408.10 annually at the beginning of each year if our account earned interest at the rate of 14.5% per year, compounded quarterly, and $470.57 if we made our contribution at the end of each year. Now let us change the interest rate to 10%. The first five rows of our model would appear as follows:

```
D4: 0.1                                                                    READY

         A         B         C         D         E         F         G         H
1                        RETIREMENT CONTRIBUTION MODEL
2
3                  AMOUNT DESIRED:       50000          CONTRIBUTION REQUIRED
4                  INTEREST RATE(%):       0.1          BEGINNING   END
5                  COMPOUNDING PERIOD        4          757.2938 835.9107
6                      WHEN DEPOSIT MADE
7                  BEGINNING OF YEAR            END OF YEAR
8            1         1.103812                     1
9            2         1.218402              1.103812
10           3         1.344888              1.218402
11           4         1.484505              1.344888
12           5         1.638616              1.484505
13           6         1.808725              1.638616
14           7         1.996495              1.808725
15           8         2.203756              1.996495
16           9         2.432535              2.203756
17          10         2.685063              2.432535
18          11         2.963808              2.685063
19          12         3.271489              2.963808
20          13         3.611112              3.271489
```

Prior to moving on to our next retirement model, let us first save the and then list its final cell contents to alleviate any confusion concerning the changes required to the formulas when we moved cells B3 through D5 to cells A3 through C5.

We can save this model by entering the command:

/File,Save,B:RETIRE1⏎

which will save the model under the filename RETIRE1 on the diskette in drive B. To display the contents of the cells of our model, we can enter the command:

/**P**rint,**P**rinter,**R**ange,**A1.G29**⏎,**O**ptions,**O**ther,**C**ell-Formulas,**Q**uit,**G**o,**P**age,**Q**uit

The results of this command are shown in figure 14.3.

```
C1:  'RETIREMENT CONTRIBUTION MODEL
B3:  'AMOUNT DESIRED:
D3:  50000
F3:  'CONTRIBUTION REQUIRED
B4:  'INTEREST RATE(%):
D4:  0.1
F4:  'BEGINNING
G4:  '  END
B5:  'COMPOUNDING PERIODS:
D5:  4
F5:  +C29
G5:  +D29
C6:  'WHEN DEPOSIT MADE
B7:  'BEGINNING OF YEAR
E7:  'END OF YEAR
A8:  1
C8:  (1+D$4/D$5)^(A8*D$5)
E8:  (1+D$4/D$5)^((A8-1)*D$5)
A9:  +A8+1
C9:  (1+D$4/D$5)^(A9*D$5)
E9:  (1+D$4/D$5)^((A9-1)*D$5)
A10: +A9+1
C10: (1+D$4/D$5)^(A10*D$5)
E10: (1+D$4/D$5)^((A10-1)*D$5)
A11: +A10+1
C11: (1+D$4/D$5)^(A11*D$5)
E11: (1+D$4/D$5)^((A11-1)*D$5)
A12: +A11+1
C12: (1+D$4/D$5)^(A12*D$5)
E12: (1+D$4/D$5)^((A12-1)*D$5)
A13: +A12+1
C13: (1+D$4/D$5)^(A13*D$5)
E13: (1+D$4/D$5)^((A13-1)*D$5)
A14: +A13+1
C14: (1+D$4/D$5)^(A14*D$5)
E14: (1+D$4/D$5)^((A14-1)*D$5)
A15: +A14+1
```

Figure 14.3. Contribution model cell contents

figure continued on following page

```
C15:  (1+D$4/D$5)^(A15*D$5)
E15:  (1+D$4/D$5)^((A15-1)*D$5)
A16:  +A15+1
C16:  (1+D$4/D$5)^(A16*D$5)
E16:  (1+D$4/D$5)^((A16-1)*D$5)
A17:  +A16+1
C17:  (1+D$4/D$5)^(A17*D$5)
E17:  (1+D$4/D$5)^((A17-1)*D$5)
A18:  +A17+1
C18:  (1+D$4/D$5)^(A18*D$5)
E18:  (1+D$4/D$5)^((A18-1)*D$5)
A19:  +A18+1
C19:  (1+D$4/D$5)^(A19*D$5)
E19:  (1+D$4/D$5)^((A19-1)*D$5)
A20:  +A19+1
C20:  (1+D$4/D$5)^(A20*D$5)
E20:  (1+D$4/D$5)^((A20-1)*D$5)
A21:  +A20+1
C21:  (1+D$4/D$5)^(A21*D$5)
E21:  (1+D$4/D$5)^((A21-1)*D$5)
A22:  +A21+1
C22:  (1+D$4/D$5)^(A22*D$5)
E22:  (1+D$4/D$5)^((A22-1)*D$5)
A23:  +A22+1
C23:  (1+D$4/D$5)^(A23*D$5)
E23:  (1+D$4/D$5)^((A23-1)*D$5)
A24:  +A23+1
C24:  (1+D$4/D$5)^(A24*D$5)
E24:  (1+D$4/D$5)^((A24-1)*D$5)
A25:  +A24+1
C25:  (1+D$4/D$5)^(A25*D$5)
E25:  (1+D$4/D$5)^((A25-1)*D$5)
A26:  +A25+1
C26:  (1+D$4/D$5)^(A26*D$5)
E26:  (1+D$4/D$5)^((A26-1)*D$5)
A27:  +A26+1
C27:  (1+D$4/D$5)^(A27*D$5)
```

Figure 14.3.(cont.)   Contribution model cell contents

figure continued on following page

```
E27:  (1+D$4/D$5)^((A27-1)*D$5)
C28:  @SUM(C8..C27)
D28:  @SUM(E8..D27)
C29:  +D3/C28
D29:  +D3/D28
```

Figure 14.3.(cont.)   Contribution model cell contents

The Growth Projection Model

The growth projection model we will develop will permit us to estimate the value of a retirement fund at some point in the future based upon fixed annual deposits and assuming a given expected interest rate funds will earn in that account.

The growth projection model will be developed using two standard annuity formulas. Similar to the contribution model previously covered, the value of our retirement fund will vary based upon whether we make into our annual deposit at the beginning of the year or at the end of each year.

The value of a retirement fund can be computed by solving the following formula when annual deposits are made at the beginning of each year.

$$\text{Fund Value} = \sum_{i=1}^{\text{Years}} \text{Annual Deposit} * (1+\frac{I}{m})^{i*m}$$

where:

Years	=	number of years to retirement
m	=	compounding periods per year
I	=	annual interest rate/100

When the annual deposit is made at the end of each year, the value of of the retirement fund can be computed by solving the following formula:

$$\text{Fund Value} = \sum_{i=1}^{\text{Years}} \text{Annual Deposit} * (1+\frac{I}{m})^{k*m}$$

where:

$k = i-1$

We can easily modify our previously developed contribution model to obtain a growth projection model. If we previously saved the contribution model we can enter the command:

/File,Retrieve,**B:RETIRE1**↵

to load it into memory, assuming it is on the diskette in drive B. In place of an amount desired, we will have an annual payment (cell C3) that will grow based upon a projected interest rate (cell C4) compounded a number of times per year (cell C5). Similarly, instead of trying to determine the contribution required, we will want to determine the fund value based upon deposits made at the beginning and the end of the year.

Assuming we want to analyze contributions over a 20-year period, we can then use the same format as our previous model. We would enter the formula +C$3*(1+C$4/C$5)^(A8*C$5) into cell C8 and copy this formula into cells C9 through C27. Since the fund value is the sum of the 20 periods, we do not require the entry previously contained in cell C29 as cell C28 contains the formula @SUM(C8.C27). As this is the fund value based upon annual contributions at the beginning of the year, we would enter +C28 into cell F5. Similarly, we would enter the formula +C$3*(1+C$4/C$5)^((A8-1)*C$5) into cell E8 and copy this formula through cells E9 to E27. Next, we would eliminate the previous entry in cell D29 and enter +D28 into cell G5, resulting in the first five rows of our model appearing as follows if we enter the command:

/Worksheet,Global,Format,Text

to display formula values.

A1:   READY

```
         A        B         C        D       E        F        G        H
1                          RETIREMENT FUND GROWTH PROJECTION MODEL
2
3    ANNUAL PAYMENT:                      FUND VALUE WHEN DEPOSITS MADE AT
4    INTEREST RATE(%):                           BEGINNING   END
5    COMPOUNDING PERIODS:                          +C28      +D28
6                          WHEN DEPOSIT MADE
7              BEGINNING OF YEAR            END OF YEAR
8          1               +C$3*(1+         +C$3*(1+
9    +A8+1                 +C$3*(1+         +C$3*(1+
10   +A9+1                 +C$3*(1+         +C$3*(1+
11   +A10+1                +C$3*(1+         +C$3*(1+
12   +A11+1                +C$3*(1+         +C$3*(1+
13   +A12+1                +C$3*(1+         +C$3*(1+
14   +A13+1                +C$3*(1+         +C$3*(1+
15   +A14+1                +C$3*(1+         +C$3*(1+
16   +A15+1                +C$3*(1+         +C$3*(1+
17   +A16+1                +C$3*(1+         +C$3*(1+
18   +A17+1                +C$3*(1+         +C$3*(1+
19   +A18+1                +C$3*(1+         +C$3*(1+
20   +A19+1                +C$3*(1+         +C$3*(1+
                                                              CAPS
```

Now let us exercise this model to verify our modifications to RETIRE1. Suppose we contribute $757.29 per year and our fund earns 10% interest, compounded quarterly. After we enter the three data elements into cells C3 through C5 and turn the formula display off with the command:

/Worksheet,Global,Format,General

we find that the first five rows of our model would appear as follows, verifying the accuracy of our program since the results are within 26¢ of

C5: 4   READY

```
         A        B         C        D       E        F        G        H
1                          RETIREMENT FUND GROWTH PROJECTION MODEL
2
3    ANNUAL PAYMENT:        757.29            FUND VALUE WHEN DEPOSITS MADE AT
4    INTEREST RATE(%):       0.1                    BEGINNING   END
5    COMPOUNDING PERIOD       4                     49999.74 45297.29
6                          WHEN DEPOSIT MADE
7              BEGINNING OF YEAR            END OF YEAR
8          1            835.9064              757.29
9          2            922.6843             835.9064
10         3           1018.470              922.6843
11         4           1124.201             1018.470
12         5           1240.907             1124.201
13         6           1369.730             1240.907
14         7           1511.925             1369.730
15         8           1668.883             1511.925
16         9           1842.134             1668.883
17        10           2033.371             1842.134
18        11           2244.462             2033.371
19        12           2477.466             2244.462
20        13           2734.659             2477.466
                                                              CAPS
```

the contribution amount we determined was required to obtain a $50,000 fund at 10% interest, compounded quarterly.

To insure that the reader correctly denotes the modifications made to the contribution model, we have listed the contents of the cells of this model as a reference guide in figure 14.4.

```
C1:  'RETIREMENT FUND GROWTH PROJECTION MODEL
A3:  'ANNUAL PAYMENT:
C3:  757.29
E3:  'FUND VALUE WHEN DEPOSITS MADE AT
A4:  'INTEREST RATE(%):
C4:  0.1
F4:  'BEGINNING
G4:  '   END
A5:  'COMPOUNDING PERIODS:
C5:  4
F5:  +C28
G5:  +D28
C6:  'WHEN DEPOSIT MADE
B7:  'BEGINNING OF YEAR
E7:  'END OF YEAR
A8:  1
C8:  +C$3*(1+C$4/C$5)^(A8*C$5)
E8:  +C$3*(1+C$4/C$5)^((A8-1)*C$5)
A9:  +A8+1
C9:  +C$3*(1+C$4/C$5)^(A9*C$5)
E9:  +C$3*(1+C$4/C$5)^((A9-1)*C$5)
A10: +A9+1
C10: +C$3*(1+C$4/C$5)^(A10*C$5)
E10: +C$3*(1+C$4/C$5)^((A10-1)*C$5)
A11: +A10+1
C11: +C$3*(1+C$4/C$5)^(A11*C$5)
E11: +C$3*(1+C$4/C$5)^((A11-1)*C$5)
A12: +A11+1
C12: +C$3*(1+C$4/C$5)^(A12*C$5)
E12: +C$3*(1+C$4/C$5)^((A12-1)*C$5)
A13: +A12+1
```

Figure 14.4. Cell contents of the Growth Projection Model

figure continued on following page

```
C13:  +C$3*(1+C$4/C$5)^(A13*C$5)
E13:  +C$3*(1+C$4/C$5)^((A13-1)*C$5)
A14:  +A13+1
C14:  +C$3*(1+C$4/C$5)^(A14*C$5)
E14:  +C$3*(1+C$4/C$5)^((A14-1)*C$5)
A15:  +A14+1
C15:  +C$3*(1+C$4/C$5)^(A15*C$5)
E15:  +C$3*(1+C$4/C$5)^((A15-1)*C$5)
A16:  +A15+1
C16:  +C$3*(1+C$4/C$5)^(A16*C$5)
E16:  +C$3*(1+C$4/C$5)^((A16-1)*C$5)
A17:  +A16+1
C17:  +C$3*(1+C$4/C$5)^(A17*C$5)
E17:  +C$3*(1+C$4/C$5)^((A17-1)*C$5)
A18:  +A17+1
C18:  +C$3*(1+C$4/C$5)^(A18*C$5)
E18:  +C$3*(1+C$4/C$5)^((A18-1)*C$5)
A19:  +A18+1
C19:  +C$3*(1+C$4/C$5)^(A19*C$5)
E19:  +C$3*(1+C$4/C$5)^((A19-1)*C$5)
A20:  +A19+1
C20:  +C$3*(1+C$4/C$5)^(A20*C$5)
E20:  +C$3*(1+C$4/C$5)^((A20-1)*C$5)
A21:  +A20+1
C21:  +C$3*(1+C$4/C$5)^(A21*C$5)
E21:  +C$3*(1+C$4/C$5)^((A21-1)*C$5)
A22:  +A21+1
C22:  +C$3*(1+C$4/C$5)^(A22*C$5)
E22:  +C$3*(1+C$4/C$5)^((A22-1)*C$5)
A23:  +A22+1
C23:  +C$3*(1+C$4/C$5)^(A23*C$5)
E23:  +C$3*(1+C$4/C$5)^((A23-1)*C$5)
A24:  +A23+1
C24:  +C$3*(1+C$4/C$5)^(A24*C$5)
E24:  +C$3*(1+C$4/C$5)^((A24-1)*C$5)
A25:  +A24+1
C25:  +C$3*(1+C$4/C$5)^(A25*C$5)
E25:  +C$3*(1+C$4/C$5)^((A25-1)*C$5)
```

Figure 14.4.(cont.)   Cell contents of the Growth Projection Model

figure continued on following page

```
A26:  +A25+1
C26:  +C$3*(1+C$4/C$5)^(A26*C$5)
E26:  +C$3*(1+C$4/C$5)^((A26-1)*C$5)
A27:  +A26+1
C27:  +C$3*(1+C$4/C$5)^(A27*C$5)
E27:  +C$3*(1+C$4/C$5)^((A27-1)*C$5)
C28:  @SUM(C8..C27)
D28:  @SUM(E8..E27)
```

Figure 14.4.(cont.)   Cell contents of the Growth Projection Model

The Consequences of Early Withdrawal

Funds build up rapidly in an Individual Retirement Account because contributions are tax free and the money grows tax free until withdrawal. Due to this, many persons are reluctant to remove funds from this type of account. In addition, since funds withdrawn prior to age 59½ are currently subject to a 10% penalty, many investors prefer to seek funds from other sources than their retirement account. Because of the 10% penalty and the concept of "locking one's funds away" for many years, less than one-quarter of all households have opened an IRA.

Although funds placed into an IRA or similar retirement account should be viewed as the establishment of a long-term savings program, in certain situations a retirement fund may prove more economically viable for a period of time than simply not establishing this type of account. In such situations, the additional income derived from the tax-deferred status of a retirement account may outweigh the taxes and penalties the investor must pay for withdrawing funds prior to the age 59½. To illustrate this concept, let us assume we have $2,000 which we could place into an IRA, however, we are not sure we would like to leave this amount in the IRA until we reach the age 59½. Thus, we might wish to know the economics associated with the withdrawal of our investment prior to reaching age 59½.

Let us assume we are in the 40% marginal tax bracket and the IRA we wish to open pays interest at the rate of 10% per year. Assuming interest is compounded annually, after 5 years our account balance would be:

$$\text{Balance} = \$2000(1+.10)^5 = \$3221.00$$

If we withdraw the funds in our retirement account at the end of the fifth year, we will have to pay taxes on the money plus the 10% penalty tax. This would reduce our proceeds as follows:

Accounts balance year five		$3,221.00
Less:		
40% federal tax	$1,288.40	
10% penalty	322.10	
Total reduction		$1,610.50
Net proceeds		$1610.50

Now let us examine the effect of not contributing the $2,000 into a retirement account. If we are in the 40% federal tax bracket, taxes would amount to $800, leaving $1,200 available for savings. If we placed the $1,200 into a regular savings account yielding 10% interest, each year 40% of the interest would be lost to taxes, reducing our net interest to 6%. After 5 years, our non-retirement account balance would be:

$$\text{Balance} = \$1{,}200(1+.06)^5 = \$1{,}605.87$$

Based upon opening an IRA and withdrawing the proceeds 5 years later, we are ahead by $4.63 compared with not opening a retirement account. It should be noted that 5 years in this example is the approximate breakeven point between having a retirement account and not having one if funds earn interest at the rate of 10% compounded annually. If we withdraw the proceeds from the retirement fund earlier than 5 years, it would have been more advantageous financially not to have opened this type of account. Similarly, the advantage of having a retirement account increases with the duration we let funds lie in that account as interest builds upon interest tax free.

CONSTRUCTING THE MODEL

We can construct a generalized model to compare investing funds in a retirement account and withdrawing such funds prior to age 59½ with an investment in a non-retirement account. The net proceeds obtained from placing funds in a retirement account can be computed from the following formula:

$$\text{Net Proceeds from Retirement Account} = (1-(F+.10))^*(D^*(1+\frac{i}{n})^{n^*y})$$

where:

F = your marginal federal tax bracket expressed as a percent
D = amount deposited into the retirement fund
i = interest rate expressed as an annual percent
n = number of compounding periods per year
y = number of years funds left in the retirement account

Similarly, we can express the net proceeds from a non-retirement account as follows:

$$\text{Net Proceeds Non-Retirement Account} = D^*(1-F)^*(1+\frac{i^*(1-F)}{n})^{n^*y}$$

where: D, F, i, n and y denote the variables previously referenced

Since we wish to compare the effect of withdrawing funds from a retirement account and paying a penalty with a taxable investment we can construct a tabular model to compare the net proceeds resulting from each type of account.

In developing our model, we will probably desire to enter and modify data concerning our marginal federal tax bracket, the amount deposited into the fund, the interest rate the deposit earns and the number of compounding periods per year. Thus, let us enter the following headings into our model:

```
A1:                                                                      READY

          A         B         C         D         E      F      G       H
1                   RETIREMENT FUND WITHDRAWAL ANALYSIS
2
3     FEDERAL TAX BRACKET:
4     AMOUNT DEPOSITED:
5     INTEREST RATE (%):
6     COMPOUNDING PERIODS:
7
8     YEAR      RETIREMENT FUND    NON-RETIREMENT FUND        GAIN/LOSS
9
10
11
12
13
14
15
16
17
18
19
20
```

Note from the preceding we will enter our data elements into cells C3 through C6 which will form the basis for our computations.

Suppose we wish to examine the consequences of early withdrawal over a 10-year period. In cell A9 we would enter the numeral 1 while we would enter the formula +A9+1 into cell A10. Now we can copy this formula through cell A18 by entering the command:

$$/\text{Copy},\textbf{A10}\text{-}\lrcorner,\textbf{A11.A18}\text{-}\lrcorner$$

which results in the numbers 1 through 10 contained in cells A10 through A18. Next, we would enter the formula:

$$(1-(C\$3+O.1))*(C\$4*(1+C\$5/C\$6) \wedge (C\$6*A9))$$

into cell B9. Since the net proceeds of the retirement account are based upon the number of years the funds remain in the account, the C3, C4, C5 and C6 values must remain absolute when we copy this formula from cell B9 into cells B10 through B18. Thus, we would enter the command to copy:

$$/\text{Copy},\textbf{B9}\text{-}\lrcorner,\textbf{B10.B18}\text{-}\lrcorner$$

For the non-retirement fund computations, we would enter the formula:

$$+C\$4*(1-C\$3)*(1+(C\$5*(1-C\$3)/C\$6)) \wedge (C\$6*A9)$$

into cell D9. Then we would copy this formula into cells D10 through D18 by entering the command:

/Copy,D9⏎,D10.D18⏎

Similar to our previous formula, only A9 is not absolute. The computation in our GAIN/LOSS column only requires us to subtract the values in column D from column B. Thus, we would enter the formula +B9-D9 into cell G9 and copy this formula through cell G18 by entering the command:

/Copy,G9⏎,G10.G18⏎

If we are entering the preceding formulas and see the messages ERR throughout our model, once again the failure to define values for the denominators in our equations has caused this to occur. As long as we have entered the equations correctly, we can ignore these messages as they will disappear when we enter our data elements into cells C3 through C6.

Let us assume we are in the 50% federal tax bracket and wish to analyze the effect of depositing $2,000 into an account earning 10% interest compounded quarterly. Based upon the following computations, we can determine the gain or loss of early withdrawal from a retirement account in comparison to depositing our funds in a conventional non-retirement account. As indicated by the results from exercising this model, as shown in figure 14.5, one would be better off financially by placing one's funds in a non-retirement account unless he or she could leave the retirement account deposit in that account for 5 or more years.

```
         A         B          C         D          E         F         G          H
 1                 RETIREMENT FUND WITHDRAWAL ANALYSIS
 2
 3   FEDERAL TAX BRACKE        0.5
 4   AMOUNT DEPOSITED:        2000
 5   INTEREST RATE (%):        0.1
 6   COMPOUNDING PERIOD          4
 7
 8   YEAR        RETIREMENT FUND      NON-RETIREMENT FUND          GAIN/LOSS
 9          1 883.0503              1050.945                       -167.895
10          2 974.7223              1104.486                       -129.763
11          3 1075.911              1160.754                        -84.8434
12          4 1187.604              1219.889                        -32.2850
13          5 1310.893              1282.037                         28.85592
14          6 1446.980              1347.351                         99.62970
15          7 1597.196              1415.992                        181.2037
16          8 1763.005              1488.130                        274.8750
17          9 1946.028              1563.943                        382.0844
18         10 2148.051              1643.619                        504.4316
19
20
```

Figure 14.5.   Results of Consequences of Early Withdrawal model

15

Fixed Income Security Tracking

Concept

Recent changes in banking regulations have resulted in numerous types of certificates of deposit being offered to savers. When coupled with Individual Retirement Accounts, Keogh accounts for the self-employed and a variety of bonds offered by brokerage firms, the individual saver has a wide range of choices in which to invest his or her savings.

Due to the competition among borrowers for the investor's savings, it is quite common for persons to have many different accounts and invest in a variety of securities. Since the minimum amount one can invest in a certificate of deposit has been lowered to $100 by many savings institutions, it is often a time consuming task to keep track of one's fixed income securities, their maturity date, annual income and other pertinent information. It is in this area that a security tracking model may be beneficial for both the small and large investor.

147

The Fixed Income Security Model

There are several items of information that are common to most fixed income securities which we may wish to include in our model. These items include the amount or value of the security, its interest rate and maturity date. Since there are many different types of securities, we may also wish to include a column that describes the particular security or the institution we purchased it from.

Although one common use of a fixed income security model is to track our securities by their maturity date for reinvestment purposes, we can also use the model to project our income from such securities. This can be accomplished by adding a column to our model that will contain the yearly income of the security. Let us initialize our model, entering the appropriate headings until it appears similar to figure 15.1.

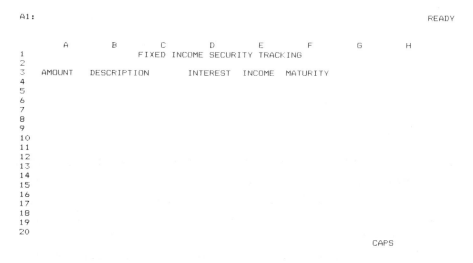

Figure 15.1. Initial headings

Note that we probably do not consider ourselves to be in the major investor category as we have left the column width settings at the 1-2-3 default value of 9 positions. We will, however, change the display format of columns A, D and E to 2 decimal digits by entering the following **/RF** commands:

/Range,Format,Fixed,2-⌐,**A1.A100**-⌐
/Range,Format,Fixed,2-⌐,**D1.E100**-⌐

The first / **RF** command will set the display format of column A to a money display while the second / **RF** command sets columns D through E to that display format, resulting in numerics being displayed with 2 decimal digits.

Note that multiplying the entry in column A by the interest rate in column C results in the income amount that will be contained in column E. Thus, we would enter the formula +A4*D4/100 into cell E4. Then, we can use the /**C** command to copy this formula into as many cells in column E as required. If we have 10 securities in our fixed income portfolio, we will enter the command:

/Copy,**E4**-⌐,**E5.E13**-⌐

to copy the formula into cells E5 through E13. Upon completion of the replication process, we could enter the command:

/Range,Format,Text,**E3.E13**-⌐

to turn the formula display on if it is not already on. Doing so would result in the contents of cells E3 through E14 appearing as follows:

```
E3:   (F2)   ^INCOME
E4:   (F2)   +A4*D4/100
E5:   (F2)   +A5*D5/100
E6:   (F2)   +A6*D6/100
E7:   (F2)   +A7*D7/100
E8:   (F2)   +A8*D8/100
E9:   (F2)   +A9*D9/100
E10:  (F2)   +A10*D10/100
E11:  (F2)   +A11*D11/100
E12:  (F2)   +A12*D12/100
E13:  (F2)   +A13*D13/100
```

To change the display format to show the results of the formulas in cells E4 to E13 as money display with two decimal places, we would enter the command:

/**R**ange,Format,Fixed,**2**↵,**E3.E13**↵

Now, let us enter the data elements into our model. While the entry of an amount, description and interest data is self-explanatory, the entry of the maturity date requires some amplification. If we enter a maturity value of 01/04/85 into cell F4 because our first security matured on January 4, 1985, 1-2-3 would first divide 1 by 4 and then divide the results of that division by 85, placing the numeric value of these arithmetic operations into cell F4. Since this is obviously not our intention, we will precede the entry of each maturity date by a single quotation mark (') to insure 1-2-3 treats the data as text. Another factor we must take into consideration prior to entering the maturity date of the security is the method by which 1-2-3 sorts if we later wish to use the /**DS** command to obtain a list of securities sorted by their maturity date. Since the sort is accomplished left to right, we must enter our data in the form of YY/MM/DD instead of the more conventional DD/MM/YY format we are probably accustomed to using.

Now, let us proceed to enter the relevant data for 10 fixed income securities, perhaps resulting in our model now appearing similar to figure 15.2.

A1: (F2)   READY

	A	B	C	D	E	F	G	H
1			FIXED	INCOME	SECURITY	TRACKING		
2								
3	AMOUNT	DESCRIPTION		INTEREST	INCOME	MATURITY		
4	500.00	FULTON FEDERAL		12.75	63.75	85/08/05		
5	5000.00	FULTON FEDERAL		14.00	700.00	87/12/08		
6	750.00	HOME FEDERAL		12.75	95.63	85/04/01		
7	800.00	HOME FEDERAL		15.00	120.00	89/12/03		
8	2000.00	PEOPLES FEDERAL		12.00	240.00	85/04/02		
9	3000.00	CENTRAL BANK		11.75	352.50	86/05/01		
10	5000.00	CENTRAL BANK		13.00	650.00	90/05/02		
11	1000.00	HOME FEDERAL		13.25	132.50	87/03/15		
12	4000.00	HOME FEDERAL		13.25	530.00	87/09/15		
13	4000.00	HOME FEDERAL		14.00	560.00	88/01/07		
14								
15								
16								
17								
18								
19								
20								

CAPS

Figure 15.2. Model after entry of security data

Since an indication of the total amount of our securities and their income might be beneficial, we can easily modify our model to obtain this information. If we wish to indicate a total for the amount and income columns, we could place a series of dashes across column A and E. To easily accomplish this task we would enter the repeat character indicator which is the backslash (\ ) followed by a dash into cell A14. Similarly, we would turn on the repeating dash in cell E14. Next, let us enter the formulas @SUM(A4.A13) into cell A15 and @SUM(E4.E13) into cell E15. Now, let us sort our securities based upon their entries in column B to illustrate a factor we must consider when sorting data in our spreadsheet. If we enter the command:

/Data,Sort,Data-Range,**A4.F13**⏎Primary-Key,**B4**⏎,**A**⏎,Go

to sort our model in ascending sequence from rows 4 through 13, our model would appear as follows:

```
A1:  (T)                                                              READY

        A          B           C          D        E         F      G        H
 1                      FIXED INCOME SECURITY TRACKING
 2
 3   AMOUNT      DESCRIPTION          INTEREST   INCOME    MATURITY
 4    3000.00  CENTRAL BANK             11.75    352.50   86/05/01
 5    5000.00  CENTRAL BANK             13.00    650.00   90/05/02
 6     500.00  FULTON FEDERAL           12.75     63.75   85/08/05
 7    5000.00  FULTON FEDERAL           14.00    700.00   87/12/08
 8    1000.00  HOME FEDERAL             13.25    132.50   87/03/15
 9     800.00  HOME FEDERAL             15.00    120.00   89/12/03
10     750.00  HOME FEDERAL             12.75     95.63   85/04/01
11    4000.00  HOME FEDERAL             13.25    530.00   87/09/15
12    4000.00  HOME FEDERAL             14.00    560.00   88/01/07
13    2000.00  PEOPLES FEDERAL          12.00    240.00   85/04/02
14   ---------                                 ---------
15   26050.00                                   3444.38
16
17
18
19
20
```

Now, let us sort our model by the maturity date of the securities. We would enter the command:

/Data,Sort,Data-Range,**A4.F13**⏎,Primary-Key,**F4**⏎,**A**⏎,Go

to sort our entries between rows 4 and 13 in ascending order, resulting in figure 15.3.

```
A1:  (T)                                                                    READY

        A        B          C         D          E        F        G        H
 1                        FIXED  INCOME  SECURITY  TRACKING
 2
 3    AMOUNT     DESCRIPTION          INTEREST   INCOME   MATURITY
 4     750.00  HOME FEDERAL             12.75     95.63  85/04/01
 5    2000.00  PEOPLES FEDERAL          12.00    240.00  85/04/02
 6     500.00  FULTON FEDERAL           12.75     63.75  85/08/05
 7    3000.00  CENTRAL BANK             11.75    352.50  86/05/01
 8    1000.00  HOME FEDERAL             13.25    132.50  87/03/15
 9    4000.00  HOME FEDERAL             13.25    530.00  87/09/15
10    5000.00  FULTON FEDERAL           14.00    700.00  87/12/08
11    4000.00  HOME FEDERAL             14.00    560.00  88/01/07
12     800.00  HOME FEDERAL             15.00    120.00  89/12/03
13    5000.00  CENTRAL BANK             13.00    650.00  90/05/02
14    ---------                                 ---------
15   26050.00                                    3444.38
16
17
18
19
20
```

Figure 15.3.   Model sorted by maturity date

If we feel we will continue to dabble in fixed income securities, it is a good idea to save our model, enabling us to easily update our portfolio when we purchase new securities or old certificates mature. If we wish to save this model on the diskette in drive B under the filename INCOME, we would enter the command:

/File,Save,**B:INCOME**◄┘

From the preceding, it should be apparent that a simple fixed income security model can assist us in managing our investments. Using this model as a foundation, the reader can easily add additional data to satisfy his or her specific requirements.

16

Discount Security Analysis

Concept

When interest rates escalate, one of the more popular types of securities investors purchase is the United States Treasury bill. This security, like commercial paper and other money market securities, is sold on a discount basis from its face value and does not pay interest directly since the return offered to investors is the difference between what he or she pays for the security and the amount received when the security matures.

One of the abnormalities of discounted securities is the fact that they are quoted in the security marketplace based upon their rate of discount and this rate of discount always understates their rate of return based upon a simple interest basis. Thus, to compare the rate of return of a discounted security such as a Treasury bill with a certificate of deposit offered by a bank or savings and loan association, one must be able to determine the simple interest rate of the discounted security.

Developing the Model

Let us examine a theoretical purchase of a $10,000 Treasury bill to understand the difference between the rate of discount and the simple interest equivalent rate offered by this type of security.

Assuming the Treasury bill is quoted at an 8 percent rate of discount, an investor purchasing a 6-month $10,000 bill would pay approximately:

$$\$10,000 - \$10,000 \times .08 \times .5 = \$9,600$$

The reason we say the investor would pay approximately $9,600 is because a 6-month bill normally matures in exactly 26 weeks or 182 days and for all discount securities the discount is based upon a year containing 360 days. Thus, the precise cost of the bill would be calculated with the following formula:

$$\text{Cost} = \text{Face Value} - \text{Face Value} \times \text{Discount Rate} \times \frac{\text{Days to Maturity}}{360}$$

To purchase the $10,000 Treasury bill, the investor must then pay:

$$\$10,000 - \$10,000 \times .08 \times \frac{182}{360} = \$9,595.56$$

Since simple interest is based upon a 365-day year, we can compute the simple interest equivalent of a discounted security with the following formula when its maturity is less than 365 days:

$$\text{Simple Interest Equivalent} = \frac{\text{Face Value At Maturity} - \text{Principal Invested}}{\text{Principal Invested}} \div = \frac{\text{Days to Maturity}}{365}$$

Upon substituting the parameters associated with our $10,000 Treasury bill example we obtain:

$$\text{Simple Interest Equivalent} = \frac{10000 - 9595.56}{9595.56} \div \frac{182}{365} = 8.45\%$$

As indicated, the simple interest rate exceeds the discount rate since the principal we invest is less than the face value of the security at maturity.

We can simplify the computation of the simple interest equivalent rate in terms of the discount rate and number of days until matures as follows:

$$i = \frac{365 \times DR}{360 - DR \times DTM}$$

where:

i = simple interest equivalent rate

DR = discount rate expressed as a percent

DTM = days until the security matures

From the preceding, there are two models we can construct that will assist us in analyzing discounted securities. First, we can construct a table that compares the discount and simple interest equivalents of different duration Treasury bills. Secondly, we can construct a model that computes the cost of a discounted security as well as its simple interest equivalent. The resulting printout of the first model might be handy to place in our desk drawer or in another appropriate place for reference while the second model will permit us to determine the precise cost and simple interest equivalent of a particular security we are interested in purchasing.

Table Construction

Suppose we wish to construct a table of the simple interest equivalent rates of 3-month (91 day) and 6-month (182 day) Treasury bills for all discount rates between 8 and 11 percent, with the discount rate incrementing by one-quarter of one percent between these values.

Let us enter the text headings that define the 3 columns of data we wish to place in our table. Thus, our initial model containing the headings for the 3 columns of data might appear as follows:

```
A1:  'T-BILL                                                         READY

          A      B      C       D      E       F       G       H
 1    T-BILL            SIMPLE INTEREST RATE
 2    DISCOUNT RATE     91 DAY  182 DAY
 3
 4
 5
 6
 7
 8
 9
10
11
12
13
14
15
16
17
18
19
20
```

Since we wish to commence the discount rate at 8 percent let us enter .08 into cell A4. To increment the discount rate by one-quarter of one percent, let us enter the formula +A4+.0025 into cell A5. Now, if we copy this formula through cell A16, we will vary the discount rate by .0025 until it reaches a value of 11 percent in cell A16. This is accomplished by the following command:

/Copy,A5↵,A6.A16↵

If we wish to see the formulas in our spreadsheet, we could move the active cell to any cell in column A and issue the commands:

/Worksheet,Column-Width,Set,13↵
/Worksheet,Global,Format,Text

and our model would appear similar to figure 16.1.

```
A1:  'T-BILL                                                            READY

              A          B          C          D        E        F        G
 1    T-BILL                     SIMPLE  INTEREST RATE
 2    DISCOUNT RATE              91 DAY     182 DAY
 3
 4           0.08
 5    +A4+0.0025
 6    +A5+0.0025
 7    +A6+0.0025
 8    +A7+0.0025
 9    +A8+0.0025
10    +A9+0.0025
11    +A10+0.0025
12    +A11+0.0025
13    +A12+0.0025
14    +A13+0.0025
15    +A14+0.0025
16    +A15+0.0025
17
18
19
20
```

Figure 16.1.   Model showing formulas

If we next enter the command:

/**W**orksheet,**G**lobal,**F**ormat,**G**eneral

to turn off the formula display, the values of 8 percent through 11 percent in increments on one-quarter of one percent will appear in our spreadsheet from cell A4 through A16 as shown in figure 16.2.

```
A1:  'T-BILL                                                            READY

              A          B          C          D        E        F        G
 1    T-BILL                     SIMPLE  INTEREST RATE
 2    DISCOUNT RATE              91 DAY     182 DAY
 3
 4           0.08
 5         0.0825
 6         0.085
 7         0.0875
 8         0.09
 9         0.0925
10         0.095
11         0.0975
12         0.1
13         0.1025
14         0.105
15         0.1075
16         0.11
17
18
19
20
```

Figure 16.2.   Model showing discount rate

Now, let us move the active cell to C4 and enter the appropriate formula to compute the simple interest rate for a 91-day security based upon the discount rate previously entered into cell A4. Since the simple interest rate is:

$$i = \frac{365 \times \text{Discount Rate}}{360 - \text{Discount Rate} \times \text{Days to Maturity}}$$

we would enter (365*A4)/(360-A4*91) into cell C4. Next we will copy the formula in cell C4 through cell C16 as follows:

/Copy,C4⤶,C5.C16⤶

This will result in the formula in cell C4 being copied from C5 through C16, with every reference to A4 adjusted. The result of this command upon the data in column C is shown in figure 16.3.

```
C1:   'SIMPLE INTEREST RATE
C2:   '91 DAY
C4:   (365*A4)/(360-A4*91)
C5:   (365*A5)/(360-A5*91)
C6:   (365*A6)/(360-A6*91)
C7:   (365*A7)/(360-A7*91)
C8:   (365*A8)/(360-A8*91)
C9:   (365*A9)/(360-A9*91)
C10:  (365*A10)/(360-A10*91)
C11:  (365*A11)/(360-A11*91)
C12:  (365*A12)/(360-A12*91)
C13:  (365*A13)/(360-A13*91)
C14:  (365*A14)/(360-A14*91)
C15:  (365*A15)/(360-A15*91)
C16:  (365*A16)/(360-A16*91)
```

Figure 16.3. Cell entries in column C after replication

Moving the active cell to D4, we would enter the formula (365*A4)/(360-A4*182) to compute the simple interest rate for a 182-day security based upon the discount rate entered in cell A4. Now, we will again use the /**C** command to copy the formula in cell D4, from cell D5 through D16 as follows:

/Copy,**D4**⏎,**D5.D16**⏎

The formulas resulting in column D would then appear as shown in figure 16.4.

```
D2:  '182 DAY
D4:  (365*A4)/(360-A4*182)
D5:  (365*A5)/(360-A5*182)
D6:  (365*A6)/(360-A6*182)
D7:  (365*A7)/(360-A7*182)
D8:  (365*A8)/(360-A8*182)
D9:  (365*A9)/(360-A9*182)
D10:  (365*A10)/(360-A10*182)
D11:  (365*A11)/(360-A11*182)
D12:  (365*A12)/(360-A12*182)
D13:  (365*A13)/(360-A13*182)
D14:  (365*A14)/(360-A14*182)
D15:  (365*A15)/(360-A15*182)
D16:  (365*A16)/(360-A16*182)
```

Figure 16.4.   Cell entries in column D after replication

This would result in the screen display as shown in figure 16.5.

```
A1:  'T-BILL                                                            READY

        A        B          C        D        E       F       G       H
 1   T-BILL               SIMPLE INTEREST RATE
 2   DISCOUNT RATE        91 DAY    182 DAY
 3
 4        0.08            0.082785 0.084529
 5        0.0825          0.085427 0.087286
 6        0.085           0.088072 0.090050
 7        0.0875          0.090721 0.092821
 8        0.09            0.093374 0.095599
 9        0.0925          0.096030 0.098385
10        0.095           0.098689 0.101178
11        0.0975          0.101352 0.103979
12        0.1             0.104018 0.106787
13        0.1025          0.106687 0.109603
14        0.105           0.109360 0.112426
15        0.1075          0.112037 0.115256
16        0.11            0.114717 0.118095
17
18
19
20
```

Figure 16.5.   Model after formula entries

To align the column of data containing the T-bill discount rate, we can use the /**RF** command as follows:

/**R**ange,**F**ormat,**F**ixed,**4**↵,**A4.A16**↵

Then, entering the command:

/**P**rint,**P**rinter,**R**ange,**A1.D16**↵,**G**o,**P**age,**Q**uit

would result in the printing of our model like that in figure 16.6.

We can save this model on disk by using the /**FS** command. Thus, we could enter the command

/**F**ile,**S**ave,**B:TBILL**↵

to save this model under the filename TBILL on the diskette in drive B. Then, we could use the /**FR** command to retrieve our model at a later date if we wish to modify our previous entries. Thus, changing cell A4 from 8 percent to 11 percent would automatically cause the two simple interest rate columns to be recomputed based upon a discount rate ranging from 11 to 14 percent.

T-BILL DISCOUNT RATE	SIMPLE INTEREST RATE 91 DAY	182 DAY
0.0800	0.082785	0.084529
0.0825	0.085427	0.087286
0.0850	0.088072	0.090050
0.0875	0.090721	0.092821
0.0900	0.093374	0.095599
0.0925	0.096030	0.098385
0.0950	0.098689	0.101178
0.0975	0.101352	0.103979
0.1000	0.104018	0.106787
0.1025	0.106687	0.109603
0.1050	0.109360	0.112426
0.1075	0.112037	0.115256
0.1100	0.114717	0.118095

Figure 16.6. Printout of model

Security Cost Computation

If we know the face value of the security, its discount rate and the number of days until it matures, we can calculate the cost and simple interest of the security.

The following model permits us to enter the three data elements into cells C3 through C5 and shows the formulas in cells F3 and F4 required to compute the cost and simple interest of the security. Remember to use the /**WE** command to clear the spreadsheet prior to entering this model if you previously entered the prior T-bill model. You will also have to use the command:

/**W**orksheet,**G**lobal,**F**ormat,**T**ext

to display the formulas.

```
A1:                                                              READY

        A        B        C        D        E            F
1                        T-BILL ANALYSIS
2
3    FACE VALUE:                  COST:           (C3-C3*C4*C5/360)
4    DISCOUNT RATE:               SIMPLE INTEREST: ((C3-F3)/F3)/(C5/365)
5    DAYS TO MATURITY:
6
7
8
9
10
11
12
13
14
15
16
17
18
19
20
```

If you turn off the formula display by entering the command:

/**W**orksheet,**G**lobal,**F**ormat,**G**eneral

"ERR" will be displayed in cell F4. You can disregard this error message as no data has been entered into cells C3 through C6 and attempting to divide by C5 in cell F4 results in infinity which causes the error message. Now, let us enter 10000 for the face value of the security, 8 percent for the discount rate and 182 days to maturity. Based upon this data, the $10,000 T-bill will cost $9,595.56 and its simple interest rate is 8.45 percent as shown below:

```
A1:                                                              READY

        A        B        C        D        E        F        G        H
1                        T-BILL ANALYSIS
2
3    FACE VALUE:              10000 COST:           9595.555
4    DISCOUNT RATE:            0.08 SIMPLE INTEREST: 0.084529
5    DAYS TO MATURITY:          182
6
7
8
9
10
11
12
13
14
15
16
17
18
19
20
```

If we wish, we can use the /**FS** command to save this model. Thus, entering:

/File,Save,B:TBILL2⏎

would save this model under the name TBILL2 on the diskette in drive B. Then, we can use the /**FR** command to retrieve this model at a later date to use it with one or more different parameters to perform a similar analysis.

17

The Effect of Interest upon Certficates of Deposit

Concept

Due to the deregulation of the banking industry, the investor now has a variety of different types of certificates of deposit to select from that were previously unavailable. Today, banks and savings and loan associations offer many types of certificates with interest compounded daily, monthly, quarterly or expressed on an annual basis, making it difficult to ascertain which investment offers the saver the greater rate of return. By using one of the models presented in this chapter, the investor can easily compare the various offerings of banks and savings and loan associations to determine which investment provides the higher rate of return when different types of compounding of interest are advertised.

Model Development

If we invest our principal denoted as P at a simple rate of interest (I) for Y years, upon maturity we would be owed:

$$P+(Y \times I \times P)$$

This can be simplified to

$$P \times (1+Y \times I)$$

Suppose we invested $100 for 1 year at a simple rate of interest of 7% payable at maturity. From the preceding formula, we would be owed

$$\$100 \times (1+1 \times .07) = \$100(1+.07) = \$107.00$$

If we assume a 2-year investment at 7%, our formula would tell us that the following payment would be received at maturity:

$$\$100 \times (1+2 \times .07) = \$100(1+.14) = \$114.00$$

Although the preceding is an accurate method of computing simple interest, in real life the first $7 of interest would be credited to our certificate at the end of the first year and the second $7 of interest would be credited at the end of the second year. If interest is credited annually, then at the end of the first year our certificate balance would be $107 and we would earn interest on the interest during the second year. Thus, when our certificate matures at the end of the second year, the payment we would receive would consist of the following:

Initial investment	$100.00
First year's interest at 7%	7.00
Second year's interest (7% on $107)	7.49
	————
Total due	$114.49

Note that the 49 cents represents interest on interest and results from the compounding of interest. In this example, we have assumed a 7% rate of interest with compounding occurring on an annual basis. Thus, the $100 invested grows to $107 at the end of the first year by multiplying the principal by 1.07 and to $114.49 at the end of the second year by multiplying the principal again by 1.07. This provides us with the formula to obtain the total value resulting from compound interest at the end of T interest periods which can be expressed as follows:

$$\text{Total Value} = Px(1+I)^T$$

Although the preceding example was based upon annual compounding, in real life the interest on a certificate or other type of bank deposit may be paid on a daily, monthly, quarterly or annual basis. The higher the frequency of compounding the higher one's account and interest is then computed on the new balance. To examine the effect of a different compounding period, let us assume that we invest $100 in a 2-year certificate at 7% compound interest and the interest is credited semiannually. Since interest is credited semiannually, each interest payment is 3.5% of the principal and we will receive four interest payments during the life of our certificate. Thus, the total value of our certificate upon maturity becomes:

$$\text{Total Value} = Px(1+I)^T = \$100x(1+.035)^4 = \$114.75$$

By changing the compound period from annual to semiannual, we find that our certificate value at maturity will increase by 26 cents. Although this may appear trivial, it does illustrate the fact that the number of compounding periods will govern our total return. Since interest rates have escalated to 15% and higher during the last few years, anyone with several thousand dollars to invest may receive an additional amount that could pay for an expensive lunch by carefully evaluating the interest rate and compounding period offered by several savings institutions and investing their funds in the institution offering the highest rate of return.

In general terms, we can express the total value of a certificate at maturity as follows:

$$\text{Total Value} = Px(1x\frac{I}{n})^{Txn}$$

where:

> P = principal amount deposited
>
> I = annual interest rate expressed as a percent
>
> n = number of compounding periods per year
>
> T = certificate duration in years

Since we must enter four data elements to obtain the total certificate value, we can construct our model to permit us to enter each element into a different cell in our spreadsheet. In the following example, we will enter the principal deposited into cell E3 while the annual interest rate will be entered into cell E4. The number of compounding periods per year will be entered into cell E5 while the duration of the certificate will be entered into cell E6. In cell E10, we will enter the formula required for the computation of the total certificate value. Here, we would enter the formula +E3*(1+E4/E5)^(E6*E5) into cell E10 as this formula represents the computation necessary to compute the total certificate value based upon the data elements of the certificate being entered into cells E3 through E6. Thus, our spreadsheet model would appear like figure 17.1.

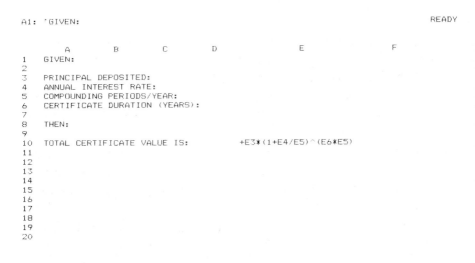

```
A1:  'GIVEN:                                                          READY

        A       B       C       D           E               F
1    GIVEN:
2
3    PRINCIPAL DEPOSITED:
4    ANNUAL INTEREST RATE:
5    COMPOUNDING PERIODS/YEAR:
6    CERTIFICATE DURATION (YEARS):
7
8    THEN:
9
10   TOTAL CERTIFICATE VALUE IS:            +E3*(1+E4/E5)^(E6*E5)
11
12
13
14
15
16
17
18
19
20
```

Figure 17.1. Model with formula display

Note that we would enter the command:

/**W**orksheet,**G**lobal,**F**ormat,**T**ext

to turn the formula display on. To widen column E we would enter the command:

/**W**orksheet,**C**olumn-Width,**S**et,**22**◄┘

if we wish to see the formula entered into cell E10. If we turn the formula display off by entering a second /**WGFG** command and reset the width of column E, the message "ERR" will be displayed in cell E10 as the printout of our model in figure 17.2 illustrates.

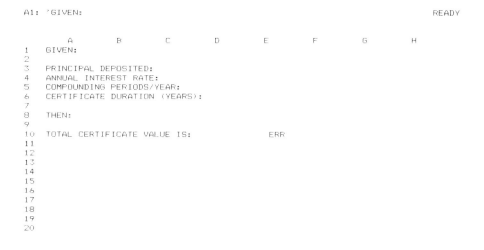

```
A1:  'GIVEN:                                                          READY

          A         B         C         D         E         F         G         H
 1    GIVEN:
 2
 3    PRINCIPAL DEPOSITED:
 4    ANNUAL INTEREST RATE:
 5    COMPOUNDING PERIODS/YEAR:
 6    CERTIFICATE DURATION (YEARS):
 7
 8    THEN:
 9
10    TOTAL CERTIFICATE VALUE IS:                        ERR
11
12
13
14
15
16
17
18
19
20
```

Figure 17.2. Model printout

This error results from the fact that the value of E5 is zero and a division by E5 in the formula intered into cell E10 results in infinity. Thus, when we enter data into cells E3 through E6 this error message will disappear and we can ignore it.

Now, let us check the accuracy of our certificate value model by entering $100 for the principal deposited, 7% for the annual interest rate,

1 for the compounding periods per year and 2 for the duration of the certificate in years. If we wish, we could also change the format of column E to display all entries with 2 decimal digits by entering the following /**RF** command:

/Range,Format,Fixed,**2**⤶,**E3.E10**⤶

Based upon entering the preceding data and the /**RF** command, our certificate model would appear as shown in figure 17.3.

```
A1:  'GIVEN:                                                              READY

         A       B       C       D       E       F       G       H
 1   GIVEN:
 2
 3   PRINCIPAL DEPOSITED:                       100.00
 4   ANNUAL INTEREST RATE:                        0.07
 5   COMPOUNDING PERIODS/YEAR:                    1.00
 6   CERTIFICATE DURATION (YEARS):                2.00
 7
 8   THEN:
 9
10   TOTAL CERTIFICATE VALUE IS:                114.49
11
12
13
14
15
16
17
18
19
20
```

Figure 17.3. Model after entry of data

Since the certificate value in our model matches the certificate value we previously computed, this example can be used as a mechanism to verify the accuracy of our model.

USING THE MODEL

Let us assume we have $100 to invest. After calling several banks and savings and loan associations, let us assume we determined the information in table 17.1 concerning the certificates of deposit offered by three institutions.

Table 17.1. Savings and loan association data

Savings Institution	Interest Rate	Duration (years)	Method of Interest Compounding
ABC	10.00	1	quarterly
ABC	10.50	2	quarterly
IJK	10.25	1	daily
IJK	10.375	2	daily
XYZ	10.375	1	quarterly
XYZ	10.400	2	quarterly

From table 17.1, it is obvious that for a 1-year investment, an interest rate of either 10.25 or 10.375 will yield a higher return than the 10% offering. This is because both the 10.25 and 10.375 securities are compounded more frequently than the security that has a 10% interest rate. Concerning the securities with an interest rate of 10.25% and 10.375%, it is not obvious which security provides the higher return. The security with the 10.25% interest rate is compounded daily while the security with the 10.375% interest rate is compounded on a quarterly basis. It is precisely for situations like this that a model which computes the total value of a certificate becomes valuable. Similarly, we may wish to analyze the 2-year certificates offered by the three savings institutions. If we compare interest rates based upon the same frequency of compounding, 10.5% on a quarterly basis provides a higher return than 10.4% on a quarterly basis. Thus, we would want to compare the total return obtained at 10.375% interest with compounding occurring on a daily basis with 10.5% interest with compounding occurring on a quarterly basis if we desire to invest in a 2-year certificate.

To accomplish our comparisons, we can either enter the new data elements into cells E3 through E6 and record the total certificate value for each entry that represents one certificate or we can copy the formula entered into cell E10 across row 10. To copy the formula, we would enter the command:

/Copy,E10↵,F10.G10↵

Since we previously changed the format of column E to 2 decimal positions, an examination of the interest rates offered by the institutions we wish to examine will reveal that they cannot fit in 2 decimal places. Thus, we should enter the command:

/Range,Format,General,E3.G10⏎

This will cause 1-2-3 to display numbers based upon their best fit in columns E through G.

After we have entered the data for the three 1-year certificates, our model would appear as shown in figure 17.4.

```
A1:  'GIVEN:                                                        READY


          A       B        C      D     E        F        G        H
  1   GIVEN:
  2
  3   PRINCIPAL DEPOSITED:                       100      100      100
  4   ANNUAL INTEREST RATE:                      0.1    0.1025  0.10375
  5   COMPOUNDING PERIODS/YEAR:                    4      365        4
  6   CERTIFICATE DURATION (YEARS):                1        1        1
  7
  8   THEN:
  9
 10   TOTAL CERTIFICATE VALUE IS:          110.3812 110.7921 110.7856
 11
 12
 13
 14
 15
 16
 17
 18
 19
 20
```

Figure 17.4. Model after entry of comparative data for 1 year certificates

An analysis of the computations of the model in figure 17.4 shows that a certificate paying 10.25% interest compounded daily results in a higher total value than a certificate paying 10.375% interest that is compounded quarterly. Although the difference appears insignificant based upon a $100 deposit, if our principal and certificate duration were to increase, the difference would become more pronounced.

Now let us investigate the three 2-year certificates. Entering these certificate parameters into the previously developed model would cause our spreadsheet to appear as illustrated in figure 17.5.

```
A1:  'GIVEN:                                                          READY


        A        B        C        D        E        F        G        H
1    GIVEN:
2
3    PRINCIPAL DEPOSITED:                             100      100      100
4    ANNUAL INTEREST RATE:                          0.105  0.10375    0.104
5    COMPOUNDING PERIODS/YEAR:                          4      365        4
6    CERTIFICATE DURATION (YEARS):                      2        2        2
7
8    THEN:
9
10   TOTAL CERTIFICATE VALUE IS:           123.0340 123.0561 122.7944
11
12
13
14
15
16
17
18
19
20
```

Figure 17.5.   Model after entry of comparative data for 2 year certificates

Now let us assume that instead of having $100 to deposit, we actually have $10,000. Here, the 2-year certificate paying 10.5% interest compounded quarterly would result in a total certificate value of $12,303.40. The certificate paying 10.375% interest would have a total certificate value of $12,305.61 while the certificate with a 10.4% interest rate would have a value of $12.279.44 upon maturity. As illustrated, the difference in the total value of the certificates is becoming more pronounced and will further deviate from one another as the duration of the certificate increases.

If we wish to save this model for future use, we can use the **/FS** command as follows:

/File,Save,**B:INTEREST**⏎

As a result of the preceding command, our model will be saved on the diskette in drive B under the filename INTEREST.

Tabular Comparison

To facilitate comparing certificates based upon their interest rate and the number of compounding periods per year, we can use 1-2-3 to create one or more tables of compound value interest factors, better known as CVIF in the financial community. Here, the CVIF shows what $1 will grow to given an interest rate compounded a number of periods per year as well as the duration for which we leave the $1 invested. Suppose we wish to construct a table of CVIF's for a 1-year security based upon interest rates from 8% to 11% varying by one-quarter of one percent with compounding periods of 1, 2, 4 and 365 times per year. To construct this model, let us first use the /WE command to clear our spreadsheet. Now, let us enter the heading INTEREST RATE into cell A3 and COMPOUNDING PERIODS PER YEAR into cell C3. Then, we would enter the digits 1, 2, 4 and 365 as text data preceded by a caret (^) to center these compounding period identifiers into cells C4 through F4.

After the preceding steps are accomplished, enter .08 into cell A5 and the formula +A5+.0025 into cell A6. Then, we can use the /C command to copy the interest rate formula through cell A17 to obtain interest rates from 8% to 11% varying by one-quarter of one percent. Thus, we would enter the command:

/Copy,A6-,A7.A17-

As a result of the copy, the contents of cells A3 through A17 would become:

```
A3:  'INTEREST RATE
A5:  0.08
A6:  +A5+0.0025
A7:  +A6+0.0025
A8:  +A7+0.0025
A9:  +A8+0.0025
A10: +A9+0.0025
A11: +A10+0.0025
A12: +A11+0.0025
A13: +A12+0.0025
A14: +A13+0.0025
A15: +A14+0.0025
A16: +A15+0.0025
A17: +A16+0.0025
```

In cell C5, we would enter the formula $(1+A5) \wedge 1$ while we would enter the formula $(1+A5/2) \wedge 2$ into cell D5. Similarly, we would enter the formulas $(1+A5/4) \wedge 4$ in cell E5 and $(1+A5/365) \wedge 365$ into cell F5. Then, we would use the /C command to copy each formula from row 5 to rows 6 through 17 of each column. As an example of one of the copy processes, column F which contains the formulas for the compound value interest factor based upon compounding 365 times per year would have the following contents:

```
F4:  ^365
F5:  (1+A5/365)^365
F6:  (1+A6/365)^365
F7:  (1+A7/365)^365
F8:  (1+A8/365)^365
F9:  (1+A9/365)^365
F10: (1+A10/365)^365
F11: (1+A11/365)^365
F12: (1+A12/365)^365
F13: (1+A13/365)^365
F14: (1+A14/365)^365
F15: (1+A15/365)^365
F16: (1+A16/365)^365
F17: (1+A17/365)^365
```

Our model will appear as shown in figure 17.6. Note that while the entries are correct, the output format does not align the data by their decimal places.

```
A1:                                                              READY


         A        B          C         D         E        F        G       H
1                          COMPOUND VALUE INTEREST FACTORS
2
3    INTEREST RATE       COMPOUNDING PERIODS/YEAR
4                           1         2         4        365
5       0.08             1.08    1.0816  1.082432 1.083277
6       0.0825         1.0825  1.084201  1.085087 1.085988
7       0.085           1.085  1.086806  1.087747 1.088706
8       0.0875         1.0875  1.089414  1.090413 1.091430
9       0.09             1.09  1.092025  1.093083 1.094162
10      0.0925         1.0925  1.094639  1.095758 1.096900
11      0.095           1.095  1.097256  1.098438 1.099645
12      0.0975         1.0975  1.099876  1.101123 1.102397
13      0.1              1.1    1.1025    1.103812 1.105155
14      0.1025         1.1025  1.105126  1.106507 1.107921
15      0.105           1.105  1.107756  1.109207 1.110693
16      0.1075         1.1075  1.110389  1.111911 1.113473
17      0.11             1.11  1.113025  1.114621 1.116259
18
19
20

                                                                CAPS
```

Figure 17.6. CVIF table

If we wish to align the data in columns C through F to 3 decimal positions, we can enter the command:

/Range,Format,Fixed,3⏎,C1.F17⏎

In order to align the data in column A, we can specify that the values be displayed with 4 decimal positions. To accomplish this, we would enter:

/Range,Format,Fixed,4⏎,A5.A17⏎

This command would cause numeric data in column A to be properly aligned. Based upon the preceding command, our table would appear as shown in figure 17.7.

```
A1:                                                                    READY

         A        B         C       D       E       F       G       H
 1                        COMPOUND VALUE INTEREST FACTORS
 2
 3   INTEREST RATE        COMPOUNDING PERIODS/YEAR
 4                           1       2       4      365
 5     0.0800             1.080   1.082   1.082   1.083
 6     0.0825             1.083   1.084   1.085   1.086
 7     0.0850             1.085   1.087   1.088   1.089
 8     0.0875             1.088   1.089   1.090   1.091
 9     0.0900             1.090   1.092   1.093   1.094
10     0.0925             1.093   1.095   1.096   1.097
11     0.0950             1.095   1.097   1.098   1.100
12     0.0975             1.098   1.100   1.101   1.102
13     0.1000             1.100   1.103   1.104   1.105
14     0.1025             1.103   1.105   1.107   1.108
15     0.1050             1.105   1.108   1.109   1.111
16     0.1075             1.108   1.110   1.112   1.113
17     0.1100             1.110   1.113   1.115   1.116
18
19
20
```

Figure 17.7. CVIF table after column alignment with border removed

Since the preceding table is based upon a 1-year period, you may wish to add this fact to the compound value interest factor heading. As an exercise, you might consider preparing a table of CVIF's for a 2-year period by modifying the equations previously entered into columns C through F, using the general formula presented earlier in this chapter to compute the total value of a certificate based upon the principal deposited, its duration, interest rate and the number of times interest in compounded per year. Here you would set the principal deposited to unity and substitute 2 for the duration and 1, 2, 4 and 365 for the compounding periods.

Prior to moving on, you may wish to save this model to diskette by entering the command:

/File,Save,B:CVIF↲

As a result of the preceding command, our model will be saved on the diskette in drive B with the filename CVIF.

18

Interest Rates
and Financial Decisions

Concept

Although several chapters in this book examine the effect of interest rates upon specific financial decisions, no discussion of spreadsheet models would be complete without examining the general effect of interest rates upon financial decisions. In this chapter, we will examine what is commonly referred to as the mathematics of finance--compound value interest factors and present value interest factors. Through an examination of the theory behind these terms, we will develop several models that can be used to easily generate tables of values that can be used in a variety of common financial situations, ranging from determining where one can obtain the highest yield on deposited funds to what payment schedule on a loan minimizes one's overall cost for the loan.

Compounding Interest Factors

To understand compound interest factors, let us assume we deposited $1,000 in a bank account that pays 10% interest compounded annually. At the end of the first year our funds are on deposit at that institution, our principal would grow mathematically as follows:

$$P_1 = P_0 + P_0 x i \text{ or } P_1 = P_0 x(1+i)$$

where:

P_0 = principal initially deposited at time 0

i = interest rate expressed as a percent

P_1 = principal value at the end of 1 period of time

In our example, $P_0 = \$1,000$ and $i = .10$, resulting in $P_1 = 1000 x (1+.10)$ or $1,100.

If we leave our funds on deposit for a second year at the same 10% interest rate, our balance at the end of that year would become:

$$P_2 = P_1 x(1+i) = P_0 x(1+i) x(1+i) = P_0 x(1+i)^2$$

Thus, at the end of year 2, our bank account balance would become $1,000x(1+.10)^2 or $1,210. The additional $10 is interest upon interest and reflects the effect of compounding. Similarly, if we left our funds on deposit for a third year, our balance at the end of year 3 would become:

$$P_3 = P_2 x(1+i) = P_0 x(1+i)^3$$

In general terms, the compound amount at the end of year n can be expressed by the equation:

$$P_n = P_0 x(1+i)^n$$

The preceding equation is the general equation of compound interest when compounding periods are once a year. When compounding periods occur more than once a year, the compound amount at the end of year n becomes:

$$P_n = P_0 \times (1 + \frac{i}{m})^{mn}$$

where: m is the number of times per year compounding occurs.

Thus, for the preceding equation, m would be 4 if the bank computes interest quarterly, 12 if the bank computes interest monthly and 365 if the bank computes interest on a daily basis.

The term to the right of P_0 in the two previously developed general compounding equations is referred to as the compound value interest factor (CVIF) in the financial community. That is, the term $(1+i)^n$ reflects the multiple a deposit will grow to based upon a given interest rate (i) and deposit duration (n) when compounding occurs on an annual basis. The term $(1+i/m)^{mn}$ reflects the multiple a deposit will grow to when compounding occurs m times per year.

Now that we have reviewed some of the basics concerning CVIF's, let us use 1-2-3 to create a table of CVIF's that we may wish to utilize to determine the potential growth of a bank deposit or certificate over a period of time. We will first assume compounding occurs on an annual basis and then modify our model to reflect the effect of compounding occurring more than once per year.

Creating the CVIF Model

Let us assume we wish to create a table of CVIF's for interest rates varying from 10% to 15% in increments of 1%. After entering the appropriate headings into our spreadsheet, we find that our model might appear as shown on the top of the following page.

To facilitate the construction of our model, we can enter the value .1 into cell B2 and the formula +B2+.01 into cell C2. Then, we merely have to copy the contents of cell C2 into cells D2 through H2. This is accomplished by the command:

/Copy, C2↵, D2.H2↵

```
A1:                                                                  READY

        A       B       C       D       E       F       G       H
1              TABLE OF COMPOUND VALUE INTEREST FACTORS
2      PERIOD
3
4
5
6
7
8
9
10
11
12
13
14
15
16
17
18
19
20
```

This will increment the interest rate by 1% in each column. After this copy
is completed, our model would appear as follows:

```
A1:                                                                  READY

        A       B       C       D       E       F       G       H
1              TABLE OF COMPOUND VALUE INTEREST FACTORS
2      PERIOD   0.1     0.11    0.12    0.13    0.14    0.15    0.16
3
4
5
6
7
8
9
10
11
12
13
14
15
16
17
18
19
20
```

To better visualize the formula entries from the previous copying, we
can enter the command:

/Worksheet,Global,Format,Text

which will result in the display of the literal data entered into the cells of our model, such as a formula or number. The result of this command is illustrated below.

```
A1:                                                                      READY

        A         B          C          D        E         F        G        H
1                 TABLE OF COMPOUND VALUE INTEREST FACTORS
2    PERIOD          0.1   +B2+0.01  +C2+0.01  +D2+0.01  +E2+0.01  +F2+0.01  +G2+0.01
3
4
5
6
7
8
9
10
11
12
13
14
15
16
17
18
19
20
```

We can easily return our display to values by entering the command:

/Worksheet,Global,Format,General

Now that we have entered our headings for the interest rates for which we wish to compute CVIF's, let us enter the periods for which we wish to compute the CVIF's. Assuming we wish a table for 15 periods, we could enter the numbers 1 through 15 into cells A3 through A17 or we could again use the copy command as a labor saving device. Assuming we wish to take advantage of the /C command, we would enter the number 1 into cell A3 and the formula +A3+1 into cell A4. Then, we would use the /C command as follows:

/Copy,A4⌐,A5.A17⌐

The results of this command are shown in figure 18.1

A1:   READY

	A	B	C	D	E	F	G	H
1		TABLE OF COMPOUND VALUE INTEREST FACTORS						
2	PERIOD	0.1	0.11	0.12	0.13	0.14	0.15	0.16
3	1							
4	2							
5	3							
6	4							
7	5							
8	6							
9	7							
10	8							
11	9							
12	10							
13	11							
14	12							
15	13							
16	14							
17	15							
18								
19								
20								

Figure 18.1. CVIF model

Now that we have completed our column and row headings, we are ready to enter the formulas necessary to compute the CVIF's. In cell B3, we would enter the formula $(1+B\$2)^{\wedge}\$A3$, as this formula reflects the compound amount at the end of period 1 based upon an interest rate of .10 or 10%. Once again we will use the / C command, this time to copy this formula into cells C3 through H3. Notice in the formula we entered into cell B3 that there are two dollar symbols ($) which are part of the reference to cells B2 and A3. The dollar symbol is significant in 1-2-3 formulas, and tells 1-2-3 that the cell reference following the dollar symbol is absolute. What this means is that when we copy the formula from cell B3 to cell C3, the cell references in the formulas will remain pointing to the absolute column or row immediately following the dollar symbol. So when we enter the command:

/Copy,B3⁻¹,C3.H3⁻¹

the actual formulas copied into cell C3 through H3 will have the cell references adjusted only in the areas that are not specified as being absolute. The formula in C3 will be $(1+C\$2)^{\wedge}\$A3$, the formula in cell D3 will be $(1+D\$2)^{\wedge}\$A3$, and so on through cell H3.

After this copy operation is completed, we will need to copy the contents of cells B3 to H3 through cells B17 to H17. To do this, we would enter the command:

/Copy,B3.H3⁻¹,B4.H17⁻¹

This copying will cause the formula in cell B3 which appears as $(1+B\$2) \wedge \$A3$ to be changed in cell B4 to $(1+B\$2) \wedge \$A4$, and in cell B5 to $(1+B\$2) \wedge \$A5$, and so on through cell H17. Once all the copy operation is completed, the values for our model will be computed and our display should appear as follows.

B3: (1+B$2)^$A3   READY

	A	B	C	D	E	F	G	H
1		TABLE OF COMPOUND VALUE INTEREST FACTORS						
2	PERIOD	0.1	0.11	0.12	0.13	0.14	0.15	0.16
3	1	1.1	1.11	1.12	1.13	1.14	1.15	1.16
4	2	1.21	1.2321	1.2544	1.2769	1.2996	1.3225	1.3456
5	3	1.331	1.367631	1.404928	1.442897	1.481544	1.520875	1.560896
6	4	1.4641	1.518070	1.573519	1.630473	1.688960	1.749006	1.810639
7	5	1.61051	1.685058	1.762341	1.842435	1.925414	2.011357	2.100341
8	6	1.771561	1.870414	1.973822	2.081951	2.194972	2.313060	2.436396
9	7	1.948717	2.076160	2.210681	2.352605	2.502268	2.660019	2.826219
10	8	2.143588	2.304537	2.475963	2.658444	2.852586	3.059022	3.278414
11	9	2.357947	2.558036	2.773078	3.004041	3.251948	3.517876	3.802961
12	10	2.593742	2.839420	3.105848	3.394567	3.707221	4.045557	4.411435
13	11	2.853116	3.151757	3.478549	3.835861	4.226232	4.652391	5.117264
14	12	3.138428	3.498450	3.895975	4.334523	4.817904	5.350250	5.936027
15	13	3.452271	3.883280	4.363493	4.898011	5.492411	6.152787	6.885791
16	14	3.797498	4.310440	4.887112	5.534752	6.261349	7.075705	7.987517
17	15	4.177248	4.784589	5.473565	6.254270	7.137937	8.137061	9.265520
18								
19								
20								

Figure 18.2. CVIF model after entry and replication of formulas

USING THE CVIF TABLE

To illustrate the utilization of the previously constructed table, let us assume we wish to determine the growth of a $1,000 deposit over a period of time, assuming an interest rate of 10%. From the preceding table, the CVIF at a 10% interest rate for period 1 is 1.1 meaning that our deposit would grow to 1.1 times its original amount or $1,100. Similarly, at the end of 5 periods the CVIF is 1.61051, meaning our deposit would grow to $1,610.51. It is interesting to note that at a 10% rate of interest compounded annually, our deposit doubles per year 7 (CVIF is 1.948717) and more than quadruples by year 15 since the CVIF is then 4.177248.

If we wish to prepare another table of CVIF's for a different range of interest rates, our modifications to the previously developed model may be reduced to a simple, one-cell change under certain situations. As an example of this, let us assume we wish a table of CVIF's based upon an interest rate ranging from 17% to 23%. Here, all one has to do is change the entry in cell B2 to .17 to obtain the desired table that is shown in figure 18.3.

```
B2:  0.17                                                                    READY

          A        B         C         D        E        F         G         H
 1               TABLE OF COMPOUND VALUE INTEREST FACTORS
 2     PERIOD      0.17      0.18      0.19      0.2      0.21      0.22      0.23
 3           1     1.17      1.18      1.19      1.2      1.21      1.22      1.23
 4           2     1.3689    1.3924    1.4161    1.44     1.4641    1.4884    1.5129
 5           3  1.601613  1.643032  1.685159     1.728  1.771561  1.815848  1.860867
 6           4  1.873887  1.938777  2.005339    2.0736  2.143588  2.215334  2.288866
 7           5  2.192448  2.287757  2.386353   2.48832  2.593742  2.702708  2.815305
 8           6  2.565164  2.699554  2.839760  2.985984  3.138428  3.297303  3.462825
 9           7  3.001242  3.185473  3.379315  3.583180  3.797498  4.022710  4.259275
10           8  3.511453  3.758859  4.021385  4.299816  4.594972  4.907707  5.238909
11           9  4.108400  4.435453  4.785448  5.159780  5.559917  5.987402  6.443858
12          10  4.806828  5.233835  5.694683  6.191736  6.727499  7.304631  7.925946
13          11  5.623989  6.175925  6.776673  7.430083  8.140274  8.911650  9.748913
14          12  6.580067  7.287592  8.064241  8.916100  9.849732  10.87221  11.99116
15          13  7.698678  8.599359  9.596447  10.69932  11.91817  13.26410  14.74913
16          14  9.007454  10.14724  11.41977  12.83918  14.42099  16.18220  18.14143
17          15  10.53872  11.97374  13.58952  15.40702  17.44940  19.74228  22.31396
18
19
20
```

Figure 18.3. CVIF model with interest rates from 17% to 23%

Since the preceding model can be easily modified to produce CVIF's for any range of interest rates, we may wish to save it. Thus, we could enter the command:

/File,Save,B:COMPOUND⏎

to save the preceding model under the filename COMPOUND on the diskette in drive B.

Suppose we wish to examine the effect of quarterly compounding upon our deposit. We would then have to change the entry in cell B3 to

$(1+B\$2/4) \wedge (\$A3*4)$. Be careful to include the second set of parentheses to insure that the term $(1+B\$2/4)$ is raised to the power of the contents of cell A3 multiplied by 4. Otherwise, if the second set of parentheses is omitted, the term $(1+B\$2/4)$ will be raised to the power of cell A3's contents and then that amount will be multiplied by 4, resulting in an incorrect value. After the preceding formula is entered into cell B3, we would use the /C command to copy it through cell H3 as follows:

/Copy,B3-⌐,C3.H3-⌐

Next, we will copy the new entries in row 3 from columns B through H through the same columns in row 17. This is accomplished by the following /C command:

/Copy,B3.H3-⌐,B4.H17-⌐

After changing the title for our CVIF table, our model would appear like figure 18.4

B3: (1+B$2/4)^($A3*4)   READY

	A	B	C	D	E	F	G	H
1		TABLE OF COMPOUND VALUE INTEREST FACTORS						
2	PERIOD	0.1	0.11	0.12	0.13	0.14	0.15	0.16
3	1	1.103812	1.114621	1.125508	1.136475	1.147523	1.158650	1.169858
4	2	1.218402	1.242380	1.266770	1.291577	1.316809	1.342470	1.368569
5	3	1.344888	1.384783	1.425760	1.467846	1.511068	1.555454	1.601032
6	4	1.484505	1.543509	1.604706	1.668172	1.733986	1.802227	1.872981
7	5	1.638616	1.720428	1.806111	1.895837	1.989788	2.088151	2.191123
8	6	1.808725	1.917626	2.032794	2.154574	2.283328	2.419438	2.563304
9	7	1.996495	2.137426	2.287927	2.448621	2.620171	2.803283	2.998703
10	8	2.203756	2.382421	2.575082	2.782799	3.006707	3.248025	3.508058
11	9	2.432535	2.655497	2.898278	3.162584	3.450266	3.763325	4.103932
12	10	2.685063	2.959873	3.262037	3.594201	3.959259	4.360378	4.801020
13	11	2.963808	3.299138	3.671452	4.084723	4.543341	5.052154	5.616515
14	12	3.271489	3.677289	4.132251	4.642189	5.213588	5.853681	6.570528
15	13	3.611112	4.098785	4.650885	5.275736	5.982713	6.782370	7.686588
16	14	3.985992	4.568593	5.234613	5.995748	6.865301	7.858395	8.992221
17	15	4.399789	5.092251	5.891603	6.814023	7.878090	9.105133	10.51962
18								
19								
20								

Figure 18.4. CVIF table after adjustment to quarterly compounding

In addition to using these tables to anticipate the growth of Individual Retirement Accounts (IRA's), Keogh plans and other retirement funds, we can also use such tables to compare the effect of interest on different types of certificates of deposit which is covered in a separate chapter in this book, we can note the difference in CVIF's between annual and quarterly compounding can be meaningful. As an example, let us consider a deposit at 10% interest over a period of 15 years. Here, the CVIF when interest is compounded quarterly is 4.399789 while it is 4.177248 when compounded annually. The difference between CVIF's is .222541, which translates into a $222.54 difference for each $1,000 one may deposit. As indicated, the mathematics of finance is an interesting subject area and by obtaining the capability to construct tables of CVIF's to meet one's particular requirements the reader should be able to perform a variety of financial analysis. Now that we have a background in the construction of CVIF tables, let us focus our attention upon another set of tables that can be equally valuable for certain types of financial analysis.

Present Value Interest Factors

Suppose we are considering leasing an automobile and after talking with two finance companies determined that our payments would be as follows, assuming yearly instead of monthly payments for simplicity.

	Easy Car Co.	Fast Wheels Inc.
Deposit	$1.000	$2,000
First Year Payment	2,400	2,200
Second Year Payment	2,600	2,200
Third Year Payment	2,600	2,200
Total	$8,600	$8,600

At first glance, it might appear that both Easy Car Co. and Fast Wheels Inc. are equal in cost, all other lease terms between the two companies assumed to be similar. However, since a dollar paid today is worth more than a dollar paid in the future, we must examine the present value of each stream of payments. Prior to doing so, let us return to the formula for compounding which for interest compounded annually is:

$$P_n = P_0 \times (1+i)^n$$

Here, the term P_0 is the initial amount deposited. Thus, finding present values is the reverse of compounding and the previous equation can be easily transformed into a present value formula as shown below.

$$P_0 = \frac{P_n}{(1+i)^n}$$

Here, the term $1/(1+i)^n$ is known in the financial community as the present value interest factor (PVIF) and many financial books contain tables of PVIF values for both annual and various compounding periods. Prior to constructing a table of PVIF's, let us first use the PVIF concept to determine which offer of the two finance companies is more financially attractive.

In our lease example, we are to make four payments. The first payment is to be made immediately, thus its PVIF is 1 or unity since there is no time difference between signing the contract and paying the deposit. For the three yearly payments, let us assume that we could earn 10% interest on our funds, thus we will use 10% as the interest rate for discounting the future payments. Thus, the PVIF for years 1 to 3 would be $1/(1+.10)^1$, $1/(1+.10)^2$ and $1/(1+.10)^3$. Since we have 1-2-3 handy, let us create a small model to compute the present value of the four payments to each finance company. Here, the formula entries for our model would appear as shown on the top of the next page, after columns A through F were widened to 12 positions with the /**WGC** command, and the format set to display formulas with the /**WGFT** command.

Note that we have multiplied each payment by the appropriate PVIF to obtain its PVIF cost. Thus, the entries in column B are multiplied by the appropriate entries in column D to obtain the PVIF cost for Easy Car. Similarly, the entries in column C were multiplied by the entries in column D to obtain the PVIF cost for Fast Wheels. Now let us use the /**WGF** command to return our model to the display of cell values by entering:

/**W**orksheet,**G**lobal,**F**ormat,**G**eneral

```
B7: @SUM(B3..B6)                                                    READY

         A              B             C             D             E             F
 1                  EASY CAR    FAST WHEELS     PVIF          PVIF COST FOR:
 2                                                          EASY CAR    FAST WHEELS
 3   DEPOSIT          1000          2000                1  +B3*D3        +C3*D3
 4   FIRST YEAR       2400          2200   1/(1+0.1)^1  +B4*D4        +C4*D4
 5   SECOND YEAR      2600          2200   1/(1+0.1)^2  +B5*D5        +C5*D5
 6   THIRD YEAR       2600          2200   1/(1+0.1)^3  +B6*D6        +C6*D6
 7   TOTAL        @SUM(B3..B6 @SUM(C3..C6            @SUM(E3..E6 @SUM(F3..F6
 8
 9
10
11
12
13
14
15
16
17
18
19
20
```

If we wish, we can also make our display more appealing by using the /**WGFF** command to have all values displayed in money format. This would be accomplished by entering the command:

/**W**orksheet,**G**lobal,**F**ormat,**F**ixed,2↵

As a result of entering the preceding commands, we find our model would then appear as follows:

```
A1:                                                                 READY

         A              B             C             D             E             F
 1                  EASY CAR    FAST WHEELS     PVIF          PVIF COST FOR:
 2                                                          EASY CAR    FAST WHEELS
 3   DEPOSIT        1000.00       2000.00       1.00       1000.00      2000.00
 4   FIRST YEAR     2400.00       2200.00       0.91       2181.82      2000.00
 5   SECOND YEAR    2600.00       2200.00       0.83       2148.76      1818.18
 6   THIRD YEAR     2600.00       2200.00       0.75       1953.42      1652.89
 7   TOTAL          8600.00       8600.00                  7284.00      7471.07
 8
 9
10
11
12
13
14
15
16
17
18
19
20
```

Based upon the preceding analysis, there exists a difference of $187.07 between the present value of the payments required by the two companies, even though their total payments are equal. Since Easy Car has the lowest PVIF cost, we would lease our automobile through that company, assuming all other items and conditions between the two firms are equivalent.

Now that we have examined the primary utilization of PVIF's-- comparing payment or receipt flows over time, let us construct a table of PVIF's. To do so we can return to either of our previously developed CVIF models and easily modify those models. Since we will be working with the formula $1/(1+i)^n$ or the formula $(1+i/m)^{mn}$ for other than annual compounding periods, all we have to do is to change the headings of our models to reflect PVIF's and then enter either formula into cell B3 and copy it through the previous boundaries used to contain the CVIF formulas.

The following table of PVIF's that is presented reflects the result of the copy of the formula $1/(1+i)^n$ into the original CVIF model presented earler in this chapter. Thus, we would first enter the formula $1/(1+B\$2) \wedge \$A3$ into cell B3 and then enter the following /C command:

/Copy,**B3**⏎,**C3.H3**⏎

Next, we would copy the formulas in row 3 from columns B through H through those columns in row 17. This is accomplished by entering the command:

/Copy,**B3.H3**⏎,**B4.H17**⏎

Once these entries are completed and we have changed our table heading, our model would appear as shown in figure 18.5.

Since as we previously noted with our CVIF model it can be a simple process to change the range of interest rates, let us save this model for future use. Thus, we could enter the command:

/File,Save,**B:PVIF**⏎

to save this model under the filename PVIF on the diskette in drive B.

B3: 1/(1+B$2)^$A3   READY

	A	B	C	D	E	F	G	H
1		TABLE OF PRESENT VALUE INTEREST FACTORS						
2	PERIOD	0.1	0.11	0.12	0.13	0.14	0.15	0.16
3		1 0.909090	0.900900	0.892857	0.884955	0.877192	0.869565	0.862068
4		2 0.826446	0.811622	0.797193	0.783146	0.769467	0.756143	0.743162
5		3 0.751314	0.731191	0.711780	0.693050	0.674971	0.657516	0.640657
6		4 0.683013	0.658730	0.635518	0.613318	0.592080	0.571753	0.552291
7		5 0.620921	0.593451	0.567426	0.542759	0.519368	0.497176	0.476113
8		6 0.564473	0.534640	0.506631	0.480318	0.455586	0.432327	0.410442
9		7 0.513158	0.481658	0.452349	0.425060	0.399637	0.375937	0.353829
10		8 0.466507	0.433926	0.403883	0.376159	0.350559	0.326901	0.305025
11		9 0.424097	0.390924	0.360610	0.332884	0.307507	0.284262	0.262952
12		10 0.385543	0.352184	0.321973	0.294588	0.269743	0.247184	0.226683
13		11 0.350493	0.317283	0.287476	0.260697	0.236617	0.214943	0.195416
14		12 0.318630	0.285840	0.256675	0.230705	0.207559	0.186907	0.168462
15		13 0.289664	0.257514	0.229174	0.204164	0.182069	0.162527	0.145226
16		14 0.263331	0.231994	0.204619	0.180676	0.159709	0.141328	0.125195
17		15 0.239392	0.209004	0.182696	0.159890	0.140096	0.122894	0.107927
18								
19								
20								

Figure 18.5.   PVIF table

It should be noted that 1-2-3 has a built-in function that can be used to calculate present values for a single payment or for a number of equal payments that represents a basic ordinary annuity.

The format of the built-in 1-2-3 function is @PV (payment, interest rate, term). As an example of the use of this function, entering the formula @PV(1, .1, 1) into any cell should result in the value of .9090909 since this represents the present value of $1 at a 10% rate of interest for 1 period of time. Since the 1-2-3 @PV function cannot be used to reflect compounding periods other than once per year, many readers may prefer to use the formulas previously covered to mathematically represent the formula they desire. In addition, since the 1-2-3 @PV function reflects an annuity of a series of even payments, one cannot use this formula to obtain any PVIF's other than for the first period at a given rate of interest.

The reader is encouraged not only to duplicate the tables of CVIF and PVIF values presented in this chapter but to prepare one or more tables that reflect the most relevant range of interest rates applicable to your circumstances, enabling you to put the mathematics of finance to work to assist you in your financial decision-making process.

19

Loan Analysis

Concept

By knowing the mathematical relationship between the cost elements of a loan, we can construct a model that will allow us to analyze most types of conventional loans.

Most conventional loan terms specify four components to include the loan amount, interest rate, loan duration and the amount of each payment. If we know three components of a loan, we can determine the fourth component based upon their mathematical relationships. The mathematical relationship of the components of a conventional loan are shown on the following page.

$$A = Px((1-(1+i)**(-N)/I)$$
$$N = -((LOG(1-IxA/P))/LOG(1+i)))$$
$$P - Ax(I/(1+(1+I)**(-N))$$

where:

A = Amount of loan

I = Interest rate per period which is the interest rate divided by the number of payment periods per year

N = Number of payment periods over the life of the loan

P = Amount of each loan payment

Furthermore, once the preceding loan components are determined, we can compute the total payments and total interest paid during the life of the loan. The mathematical formulas required to compute these two loan factors are:

Total Payments = PxN

Total Interest = Total Payments - A

Based upon the preceding formulas, let us develop a model to analyze loans. Our initial model will be constructed to let us enter our data into cells C3 through C7 and place the results of our computations into cells F3 through F9. This is indicated by the printout in figure 19.1 showing the headings placed into our model.

In cell F3, we would enter the formula +C7*((1-(1+C4/C6) ^(-C5))/ (C4/C6)). If we want to round the result of our computation to two decimal places, we could enter the formula @ROUND(C7*((1-(1+C4/C6) ^ (-C5))/(C4/C6)),2) into cell F3 instead of the previous formula. Readers concerned about obtaining complete loan accuracy to the nearest penny will want to round all formula entries to two digits.

If we want, we could specify the interest rate per payment period in cell F4 instead of simply placing the interest rate previously entered into cell C4 into cell F4. Thus, we could enter the formula +C4/C6 into cell F4.

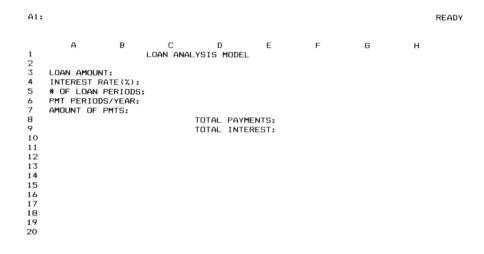

```
         A        B        C        D        E        F        G        H
1                          LOAN ANALYSIS MODEL
2
3    LOAN AMOUNT:
4    INTEREST RATE(%):
5    # OF LOAN PERIODS:
6    PMT PERIODS/YEAR:
7    AMOUNT OF PMTS:
8                          TOTAL PAYMENTS:
9                          TOTAL INTEREST:
10
11
12
13
14
15
16
17
18
19
20
```

Figure 19.1. Model headings

To compute the number of loan periods, we would enter the formula
-((@LOG(1-F4*C3/C7))/(@LOG(1+F4))) into cell F5. Note that instead
of dividing the interest rate (C4) by the number of payment periods per
year (C6), we can simply specify the value of cell F4 in our formula.

To obtain the amount of each payment, we would enter the formula
+C3*(F4/(1-(1+F4) ^(-C5))) into cell F7. Finally, we would enter the
formula +F7*F5 into cell F8 and +F8-F3 into cell F9.

The contents of cells F3 through F9 would then appear as follows:

```
F3:   +C7*((1-(1+C4/C6)^(-C5))/(C4/C6))
F4:   +C4/C6
F5:   -((@LOG(1-F4*C3/C7))/(@LOG(1+F4)))
F7:   +C3*(F4/(1-(1+F4)^(-C5)))
F8:   +F7*F5
F9:   +F8-F3
```

Our model will display six error messages as the printout in figure 19.2
illustrates.

```
A1:                                                                    READY

         A        B        C        D        E        F        G        H
1                          LOAN ANALYSIS MODEL
2
3    LOAN AMOUNT:                                          ERR
4    INTEREST RATE(%):                                     ERR
5    # OF LOAN PERIODS:                                    ERR
6    PMT PERIODS/YEAR:
7    AMOUNT OF PMTS:                                       ERR
8                                  TOTAL PAYMENTS:         ERR
9                                  TOTAL INTEREST:         ERR
10
11
12
13
14
15
16
17
18
19
20
```

Figure 19.2.   Model after entry of formulas

We can ignore these error messages as they result from the absence of values in cells C3 through C7 that are required to prevent an attempted division by zero in the formulas we previously entered into cell F3 through F8 that require the values of cells C3 through C7.

Now we are ready to exercise the model entering values for cells C3 through C6. Assuming we wish to borrow $50,000 for 20 years with interest at 17%, with payments made monthly, we would enter 50000, .17, 240 and 12 into cells C3 through C6, resulting in the computation of the amount of each payment being 733.40 as illustrated in figure 19.3.

Although we still have three ERR indications in our model, these result from the references to cell C7 in the formulas entered in cells F5, F8 and F9. Since we just computed the amount of each payment, we can now enter that value into cell C7 to complete our calculations as indicated in figure 19.4.

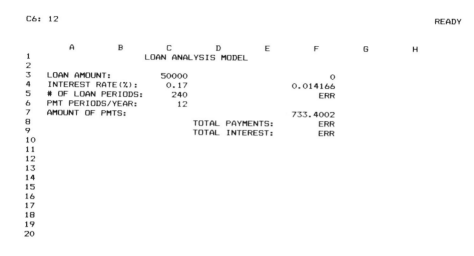

Figure 19.3. Model after entries into cells C3 through C6

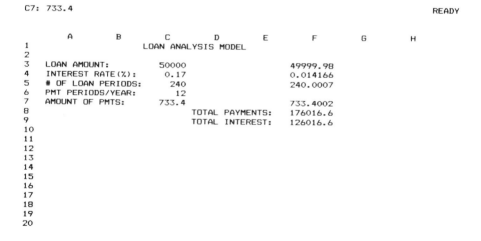

Figure 19.4. Model after entry of value in C7

Modifications to Consider

If we want a schedule of payments we can use the preceding model as the foundation for developing an amortization schedule. This type of schedule would show the original balance for each payment period, the payment, interest for the period and the new balance at the end of each period. The following portion of our model illustrates how we could begin to generate the formulas necessary to compute the amortization schedule.

```
A14:                                                              READY

        A        B        C        D        E         F      G
10
11   ORIGINAL BALANCE   PAYMENT  INTEREST NEW BALANCE
12   +C3                 +C7      +A12*F4  +A12-(C12-D12)
13   +E12                +C7      +A13*F4  +A13-(C13-D13)
14
15
16
17
18
19
20
21
22
23
24
25
26
27
28
29
```

Since the original loan balance is entered into cell C3, we would enter +C3 into cell A12. Next, we would enter +C7 into C12 as this is the payment we would make each period. The interest paid each period is the product of the original balance times the interest rate per period computed in cell F4. Thus, we would enter +A12*F4 into cell D12. Since the new balance is the difference between the original balance and the principal repaid, we can first calculate the principal repayment by subtracting the interest from the payment. Then, we would subtract this amount from the original balance. Thus, we would enter the formula +A12-(C12-D12) into cell E12.

Once the new balance is computed, it becomes the original balance for the next period. Thus, we would enter +E12 into A13. Our payment remains constant in a conventional loan so we would enter +C7 into cell

C13. Next, we would enter +A13*F4 into cell D13 since the interest is computed on the loan balance at the beginning of the period. Finally, we would enter the formula +A13-(C13-D13) into cell E13 to compute the new balance.

Entering these values would result in our model appearing as shown in figure 19.5.

```
A1:                                                                    READY

          A        B        C        D       E       F       G       H
1                           LOAN ANALYSIS MODEL
2
3     LOAN AMOUNT:          50000                   49999.98
4     INTEREST RATE(%):     0.17                    0.014166
5     # OF LOAN PERIODS:    240                     240.0007
6     PMT PERIODS/YEAR:      12
7     AMOUNT OF PMTS:       733.4                   733.4002
8                                   TOTAL PAYMENTS: 176016.6
9                                   TOTAL INTEREST: 126016.6
10
11    ORIGINAL BALANCE  PAYMENT  INTEREST NEW BALANCE
12        50000              733.4 708.3333 49974.93
13    49974.93               733.4 707.9782 49949.51
14
15
16
17
18
19
20
```

Figure 19.5.   Model with modifications for amortization

As an exercise, the reader might consider copying the formulas in row 13 through row 21 to develop a 10-year amortization schedule or through row 31 to completely amortize the 20-year loan previously analyzed.

20

Net Worth Statement

Concept

One of the major requirements of most loan applications is the submission of a net worth statement or the completion of a loan form that provides the lender with this information. In this chapter, we will develop the basic format of a net worth statement that can be modified by the reader to reflect your particular circumstances. Even if you do not antici-pate taking out a loan, this model can be used as a guide for determining one's net worth and should prove to be a valuable addition to a library of models maintained by most spreadsheet users.

Developing the Model

The net worth of an individual or organization is defined as assets minus liabilities. Thus, to develop a net worth statement we can develop a list of assets in one column of our spreadsheet model and a second column of liabilities. Then, we would sum the values in each column and subtract the total liabilities from the total assets.

The assets column is basically a list of items we own, even if we have not completely paid for the item. Thus, we would include such items as cash on hand and our checking account balance as well as the value of automobiles and our home in this column. The liability column would contain a list of bills and tax payments we owe as well as the balance on loans for our home or automobiles.

Since few individuals or institutions have very similar financial circumstances, the model we will present in this chapter should be used as a guide to develop one's net worth statement. Readers may have additional assets or liabilities that can be included in this model to develop one's net worth statement. In addition, once the model is developed and saved, it becomes a simple process to modify the statement as our financial situation changes.

Our net worth model will be constructed to permit us to enter the value of our assets in column D and our obligations in column H. If our model is constructed as illustrated in figure 20.1, we will enter the formula @SUM(D5.D34) into cell D36 to obtain the total value of our assets. Next, we will enter the formula @SUM(H3.H31) into cell H36 to obtain the total amount of our liabilities. The third and final formula that is required would be +D36-H36 which computes our net worth and is entered into cell H38.

Notice that only 20 rows of the spreadsheet can be shown on the screen at any one time. The model illustrated is two screens, the first showing rows 1 through 20, and the second showing rows 21 through 40.

A1:   READY

```
          A         B         C         D         E         F         G         H
 1              NET WORTH STATEMENT FOR MR. JOHN SMITH AS OF XX/YY/ZZ
 2
 3            ASSETS                       LIABILITIES
 4   CASH:                                 CURRENT OBLIGATIONS
 5    Cash on hand                          Rent
 6    Checking Account Balance              Utilities
 7    Savings Account Balance               Insurance Premiums
 8    Money Market Fund                     Charge Card Balances
 9    Life Insurance Cash Value             Pest Control
10   MARKETABLE SECURITIES:                 Alimony
11    Stocks                                Child Support
12    Bonds                                 Other Bills
13    US Govt. Securities                  TAXES
14    Mutual Funds                          Federal
15    Other Securities                      State
16   PERSONAL PROPERTY                      Local
17    Automobiles                           Property
18    Home Furnishings                      Other
19    Clothing                             MORTGAGES
20    Jewelry                               Home
21    Stamp, Coin Collections               Rental Property
22    Other Possessions                     Other
23   REAL ESTATE                           LOANS
24    Home                                  Automobiles
25    Rental Property                       Education
26    Other Investments                     Equipment
27   PENSION                                Home Improvement
28    Vested Portion of Company Plan        Individual
29    IRA Account Balance                   Life Insurance
30    Keogh Account Balance                 Other
31   OTHER ASSETS
32    Equity in Business
33    Equipment
34    Other
35
36   TOTAL ASSETS:            0 TOTAL LIABILITIES:                0
37
38                             NET WORTH:                        0
39
40
```

Figure 20.1.   Net Worth Statement model

Prior to actually entering data into our model, we should consider the number of positions and display format of columns D and H. Since 1-2-3 initially allocates 9 positions to each column, if any one entry or an aggregate total is expected to exceed 9 digits, we should change the column width. In addition, we will probably want to display our entries in a money format with 2 digits displayed after the decimal point. Suppose we believe 12 positions are sufficient for the display of our financial data. We would then enter the following commands:

/**W**orksheet,**C**olumn-Width,**S**et,**12**↵

/**W**orksheet,**G**lobal,**F**ormat,**F**ixed,**2**↵

with the active cell positioned at any cell in the column we wish to change to set the width of columns D and H to 12 positions and display entries in those columns with 2 positions after the decimal point.

After entering our data elements, we can print our net worth statement by entering the command:

/Print,Printer,Range,A1.H40⏎,Go,Page,Quit

Then, the printed version of our net worth statement would be suitable as an attachment to a loan document or we can use it to assist us in completing a loan application.

We can print our Net Worth Statement in a condensed print mode by telling 1-2-3 to place the printer in compressed mode prior to printing. This is done by entering a printer setup string in the Option area of the /PP command. Assuming that we have an Epson MX-80 printer, the control code for compressed print is a 015. The correct command to print our model in compressed mode could be entered as:

/Print,Printer,Range,A1.H40⏎,Options,Setup,\015⏎,Margins,
Right,132⏎,Quit,Go,Page,Quit

Notice that we also had to reset the right margin to 132 positions in order to have the entire model print on one page. If we did not reset the right margin, the default of 72 print positions would have forced part of the model to print on a second page.

After we have taken the time to construct our net worth model, we should save it to facilitate its updating as our financial circumstances change. Thus, we might enter the command:

/File,Save,B:NETWORTH⏎

to save our previously constructed model on the diskette in drive B under the filename NETWORTH.

NET WORTH STATEMENT FOR MR. JOHN SMITH AS OF XX/YY/ZZ

ASSETS		LIABILITIES	
CASH:		CURRENT OBLIGATIONS	
Cash on hand	22.00	Rent	200.00
Checking Account Balance	450.00	Utilities	50.00
Savings Account Balance	8567.00	Insurance Premiums	450.00
Money Market Fund	54321.00	Charge Card Balances	27.75
Life Insurance Cash Value	4000.00	Pest Control	12.00
MARKETABLE SECURITIES:		Alimony	
Stocks	23456.00	Child Support	
Bonds	32124.00	Other Bills	
US Govt. Securities	3333.00	TAXES	
Mutual Funds	4444.00	Federal	500.00
Other Securities	333.00	State	200.00
PERSONAL PROPERTY		Local	
Automobiles	8000.00	Property	
Home Furnishings	22000.00	Other	
Clothing	1000.00	MORTGAGES	
Jewelry	2000.00	Home	67987.00
Stamp, Coin Collections		Rental Property	
Other Possessions		Other	
REAL ESTATE		LOANS	
Home	75000.00	Automobiles	7000.00
Rental Property		Education	2750.00
Other Investments		Equipment	
PENSION		Home Improvement	1250.00
Vested Portion of Company	2000.00	Individual	
IRA Account Balance	4000.00	Life Insurance	
Keogh Account Balance		Other	
OTHER ASSETS			
Equity in Business			
Equipment			
Other			
TOTAL ASSETS:	245050.00	TOTAL LIABILITIES:	80426.75
		NET WORTH:	164623.25

Figure 20.2. Net Worth Statement printout

21

Security Portfolio Analysis

Concept

Many investors keep a log of their security transactions on paper, updating the price and value of each security on a periodic basis. By developing a security model using our spreadsheet program, we can automate our record keeping process as well as obtain a mechanism for updating our security transactions as they occur.

In this chapter, we will first develop a basic stock portfolio model and then expand this model to illustrate how it can be used to develop a model to track the price of securities over a period of time. Finally, we will examine how we can obtain a visual illustration of the fluctuations in the prices of our securities by using the graphing capability of 1-2-3.

The Stock Portfolio Model

The initial stock portfolio model we will develop will be designed to provide us with an evaluation of the status of our investments at a particular point in time. The frequency with which we review our portfolio is at the discretion of the user. While some of us may wish to conduct a monthly review, others may wish to perform a weekly or daily analysis. If we date each analysis, we can combine a number of individual reviews into a tracking review which will be covered later in this chapter.

Let us assume that for our initial model we wish to include the stock name, the number of shares purchased, the purchase price per share and the dividend per share. Since we will periodically examine our portfolio based upon current market conditions, we will include a column into which we will enter the current price of the stock.

For evaluation purposes, we will compare the cost of the stock to its present market value. This will provide us with an indication of our potential gain or loss at a certain period in time. In addition, we may desire to know our expected annual income and the yield of the security based upon its current price.

Based upon the preceding, we can construct a table that will facilitate building our model. In this table, we will indicate the contents of each column and the calculations based upon the data in other columns necessary to obtain the data for calculated columns. In addition, since 1-2-3's default column width is 9 positions, we might also wish to consider the effect of the column headings upon the column width. If we wish to change the format of one or more columns, we can also include this information in our table, allowing us to easily construct our initial model. Let us assume that based upon our analysis we developed table 21.1.

In table 21.1, the term default under the column format heading indicates that the standard or default 1-2-3 format is acceptable. This means that text is left justified, numerics are right justified, numbers are displayed as an integer if the number is an integral value and numbers larger than the column width are displayed in exponential format. Since the column width that contains the number of shares is 9 positions, unless we purchase lots of penny stocks the default format should be sufficient. The dollar sign under the column format heading indicates that the numbers in these columns should be displayed with 2 digits after the

Table 21.1.   Stock portfolio data elements

Column	Contents	Calculations	Heading	Column Width	Column Format
A	Stock name	-	STOCK-NAME	15	Default
B	Number of shares	-	#-SHARES	9	Default
C	Dividend per share	-	DIVIDEND PER SHARE	9	Default
D	Cost per share	-	COST/ SHARE	9	3 decimal places
E	Current price per share	-	MARKET PRICE	9	3 decimal places
F	Total cost	B*D	TOTAL COST	10	$
G	Market value	B*E	MARKET VALUE	10	$
H	Potential gain or loss	G-F	POTENTIAL GAIN/LOSS	10	$
I	Annual income	B*C	ANNUAL INCOME	9	$
J	Current yield	(C/E)*100	CURRENT YIELD	9	3 decimal places

decimal point. Since securities such as stocks and bonds are priced in terms of eighths, we will require 3 decimal places for columns D and E to correctly display the cost and current price of the security.

We can change the width of each column from 1-2-3's default value of 9 to the number in the table by using the **/WCS** command. Thus, to change the width of column A to 15 positions we would move the active cell to column A and enter the command:

/**W**orksheet,**C**olumn-Width,**S**et,**15**↵

In a similar manner, we would change the width of column F to 10 positions by moving the active cell to column F and using 10 for the number in a second **/WCS** command and so on.

To change the format of a single column or range of columns, we will use the **/RF** command. Since we wish to set column C and F through I to a money display with 2 digits after the decimal point, we will enter the following commands:

/Range,Format,Fixed,2⤶,C1.C20⤶
/Range,Format,Fixed,2⤶,F1.I20⤶

Here, the first /**RF** command would set column C to a money display while the second /**RF** command would set columns F through I to that display mode.

Now we would enter the commands:

/Range,Format,Fixed,3⤶,D1.E20⤶
/Range,Format,Fixed,3⤶,J1.J20⤶

The preceding commands would inform 1-2-3 to set the format of columns D through E and J to display 3 decimal places.

Now that we have changed our column widths and formats to reflect the data they will contain, let us enter the headings into our model. Our initial model would then appear as follows:

```
A1:                                                              READY

             A          B          C        D         E        F         G
  1
  2    STOCK-NAME   #-SHARES   DIVIDEND   COST/    MARKET    TOTAL    MARKET
  3                            PER SHARE  SHARE    PRICE     COST     VALUE
  4    ------------------------------------------------------------------------
  5
  6
  7
  8
  9
 10
 11
 12
 13
 14
 15
 16
 17
 18
 19
 20
```

```
E1:  (F3)                                                              READY

          E          F          G          H          I          J          K
 1
 2     MARKET     TOTAL      MARKET    POTENTIAL   ANNUAL     CURRENT
 3     PRICE      COST       VALUE     GAIN/LOSS   INCOME     YIELD
 4     ----------------------------------------------------------------------
 5
 6
 7
 8
 9
10
11
12
13
14
15
16
17
18
19
20
```

A few notes may be in order concerning the headings entered into our model. First, to place the appropriate heading into the center or near center of a cell, you should enter the heading preceded by a caret mark (^). To obtain the line across row 4, we can enter a single backslash (\ ) followed by a dash into cell A4. This will cause the dash to be repeated across cell A4. We may then copy this line of dashes with the command:

/Copy,A4↵,B4.J4↵

Since 98 print positions are required to display the headings across columns A through J, if your printer does not normally print more than 80 columns across, you must enable its compressed print mode if it has one to obtain a hard copy of the model as an entity. To place a printer into compressed print mode, one must initialize a setup string for the spread-sheet to send to the printer before printing begins. We must also reset the right margin and page length. Thus, we would enter the command:

/Print,Printer,Options,Setup, \ 015↵,Margins,
Right,136↵,Page-Length,88↵,Quit,Quit

In this example, we are using the Epson MX80 printer and we would enter the " \015" as the code that places the Epson printer into compressed mode printing. We may next inform 1-2-3 to print the range bounded by cells A1 and J5 to the printer using the previously set print specification by issuing the command:

/Print,Printer,Range,A1.J5↵,Go,Page,Quit

Now let us focus our attention upon the formulas required to be entered into our model. The first item we must compute is the total cost of each stock which is the product of the number of shares times the cost per share, or simply column B times column D of each row. If we wish to enter 10 stocks into our model we can enter +B5*D5 into cell F5 and copy this formula into cells F6 through F14 as follows:

/Copy,F5↵,F6.F14↵

As a result of this copying, the contents of cells F2 through F14 would become:

```
F2:   (F2)  ^TOTAL
F3:   (F2)  ^COST
F4:   \-
F5:   (F2)  +B5*D5
F6:   (F2)  +B6*D6
F7:   (F2)  +B7*D7
F8:   (F2)  +B8*D8
F9:   (F2)  +B9*D9
F10:  (F2)  +B10*D10
F11:  (F2)  +B11*D11
F12:  (F2)  +B12*D12
F13:  (F2)  +B13*D13
F14:  (F2)  +B14*D14
```

Since the market value is the product of the number of shares times the current price per share we would enter the formula +B5*E5 into cell G5. Then we would copy this formula into cells G6 through G14 using the command:

/Copy,G5↵,G6.G14↵

Similarly, we would enter the formulas +G5-F5 into cell H5, +B5*C5 into cell I5 and (C5/E5)*100 into cell J5 and copy each formula through row 14.

Once the five preceding formulas have been entered into the appropriate cells and copied through row 14, our formula entries can be displayed by entering the command:

/Range,Format,Text,F5.J14↵

and will appear as shown in figure 21.1.

```
E5:  (F3)                                                              READY


          E           F           G           H           I           J          K
1
2     MARKET       TOTAL       MARKET    POTENTIAL     ANNUAL     CURRENT
3     PRICE         COST        VALUE    GAIN/LOSS     INCOME       YIELD
4     ----------------------------------------------------------------------
5                 +B5*D5      +B5*E5      +G5-F5      +B5*C5     (C5/E5)*
6                 +B6*D6      +B6*E6      +G6-F6      +B6*C6     (C6/E6)*
7                 +B7*D7      +B7*E7      +G7-F7      +B7*C7     (C7/E7)*
8                 +B8*D8      +B8*E8      +G8-F8      +B8*C8     (C8/E8)*
9                 +B9*D9      +B9*E9      +G9-F9      +B9*C9     (C9/E9)*
10                +B10*D10    +B10*E10    +G10-F10    +B10*C10   (C10/E10
11                +B11*D11    +B11*E11    +G11-F11    +B11*C11   (C11/E11
12                +B12*D12    +B12*E12    +G12-F12    +B12*C12   (C12/E12
13                +B13*D13    +B13*E13    +G13-F13    +B13*C13   (C13/E13
14                +B14*D14    +B14*E14    +G14-F14    +B14*C14   (C14/E14
15
16
17
18
19
20
```

Figure 21.1. Model after replication of formula entries

Note that we cannot see all the formula in column J because the width of the column is only 9 positions.

If we turn the formula display off by entering the commands:

/Range,Format,Fixed,2↵,F5.I14↵
/Range,Format,Fixed,3↵,J5.J14↵

we will see a column or error messages in column J. We can ignore these error messages as they are caused by the divisor in each formula having a value of zero since we have not entered any values into our model at this time. Since a zero divisor results in infinity, the error messages will disappear once we enter the current price of our stocks into column E.

Since our model is in excess of 80 columns, we may wish to lock column A into place to prevent the stock name from scrolling off the screen if we wish to view the column that is initially off our screen. To accomplish this, we must first enter the stock names into column A, then position the active cell to the top of column B and use the /**WTV** command as follows:

/**W**orksheet,**T**itles,**V**ertical

The preceding command will cause column A to scroll vertically but not horizontally. Now let us enter the data for the 10 stocks in our portfolio, resulting in our model appearing as in figure 21.2.

Again, we cannot view all of the spreadsheet on the screen at one time, so we can move the active cell to the right to column K to see the remainder of the model.

Although our model is completely filled in, it lacks appropriate totals for several columns. We can use the 1-2-3 @SUM function to accumulate totals for the entries in columns F through I. Thus, we would enter the formula @SUM(F5.F14) into cell F16, @SUM(G5.G14) into cell G16 and so on. We can obtain the total yield of our portfolio by dividing the total annual income by the total market value. Thus, we would enter the formula (I16/G16)*100 into cell J16 to obtain the current yield of our securities based upon their current price, resulting in our model appearing as shown in figure 21.3.

B1:   READY

	A	B	C	D	E	F	G
1							
2	STOCK-NAME	#-SHARES	DIVIDEND	COST/	MARKET	TOTAL	MARKET
3			PER SHARE	SHARE	PRICE	COST	VALUE
4	--
5	Abbet Corp.	100	1.20	52.375	54.000	5237.50	5400.00
6	Barber Inc.	50	2.65	23.750	26.500	1187.50	1325.00
7	Carlton Mfg.	50	1.30	17.250	30.875	862.50	1543.75
8	Davidson Inc.	30	1.80	16.750	17.500	502.50	525.00
9	Diskco Corp.	75	0.50	8.250	8.000	618.75	600.00
10	Dummy Motors	100	2.50	27.500	19.875	2750.00	1987.50
11	General Brick	200	0.25	5.875	4.750	1175.00	950.00
12	Tbird Roofing	50	1.50	12.625	14.000	631.25	700.00
13	Zebra Motors	50	1.25	18.375	18.375	918.75	918.75
14	Zulta Electric	300	3.75	22.500	21.750	6750.00	6525.00
15							
16							
17							
18							
19							
20							

K5:   READY

	A	F	G	H	I	J	K
1							
2	STOCK-NAME	TOTAL	MARKET	POTENTIAL	ANNUAL	CURRENT	
3		COST	VALUE	GAIN/LOSS	INCOME	YIELD	
4	---
5	Abbet Corp.	5237.50	5400.00	162.50	120.00	2.222	
6	Barber Inc.	1187.50	1325.00	137.50	132.50	10.000	
7	Carlton Mfg.	862.50	1543.75	681.25	65.00	4.211	
8	Davidson Inc.	502.50	525.00	22.50	54.00	10.286	
9	Diskco Corp.	618.75	600.00	-18.75	37.50	6.250	
10	Dummy Motors	2750.00	1987.50	-762.50	250.00	12.579	
11	General Brick	1175.00	950.00	-225.00	50.00	5.263	
12	Tbird Roofing	631.25	700.00	68.75	75.00	10.714	
13	Zebra Motors	918.75	918.75	0.00	62.50	6.803	
14	Zulta Electric	6750.00	6525.00	-225.00	1125.00	17.241	
15							
16							
17							
18							
19							
20							

Figure 21.2. Model after stock data entry

B1:   READY

```
          A          B         C         D         E         F         G
1
2   STOCK-NAME     #-SHARES  DIVIDEND   COST/    MARKET    TOTAL     MARKET
3                            PER SHARE  SHARE    PRICE     COST      VALUE
4   ---------------------------------------------------------------------
5   Abbet Corp.      100      1.20     52.375    54.000   5237.50   5400.00
6   Barber Inc.       50      2.65     23.750    26.500   1187.50   1325.00
7   Carlton Mfg.      50      1.30     17.250    30.875    862.50   1543.75
8   Davidson Inc.     30      1.80     16.750    17.500    502.50    525.00
9   Diskco Corp.      75      0.50      8.250     8.000    618.75    600.00
10  Dummy Motors     100      2.50     27.500    19.875   2750.00   1987.50
11  General Brick    200      0.25      5.875     4.750   1175.00    950.00
12  Tbird Roofing     50      1.50     12.625    14.000    631.25    700.00
13  Zebra Motors      50      1.25     18.375    18.375    918.75    918.75
14  Zulta Electric   300      3.75     22.500    21.750   6750.00   6525.00
15
16                                              TOTALS:  20633.75  20475.00
17
18
19
20
```

J16: (F3) (I16/G16)*100   READY

```
          A          E         F         G         H         I         J
1
2   STOCK-NAME     MARKET    TOTAL     MARKET    POTENTIAL  ANNUAL   CURRENT
3                  PRICE     COST      VALUE     GAIN/LOSS  INCOME   YIELD
4   ---------------------------------------------------------------------
5   Abbet Corp.    54.000   5237.50   5400.00    162.50    120.00    2.222
6   Barber Inc.    26.500   1187.50   1325.00    137.50    132.50   10.000
7   Carlton Mfg.   30.875    862.50   1543.75    681.25     65.00    4.211
8   Davidson Inc.  17.500    502.50    525.00     22.50     54.00   10.286
9   Diskco Corp.    8.000    618.75    600.00    -18.75     37.50    6.250
10  Dummy Motors   19.875   2750.00   1987.50   -762.50    250.00   12.579
11  General Brick   4.750   1175.00    950.00   -225.00     50.00    5.263
12  Tbird Roofing  14.000    631.25    700.00     68.75     75.00   10.714
13  Zebra Motors   18.375    918.75    918.75      0.00     62.50    6.803
14  Zulta Electric 21.750   6750.00   6525.00   -225.00   1125.00   17.241
15
16                 TOTALS:  20633.75  20475.00  -158.75   1971.50    9.629
17
18
19
20
```

Figure 21.3. Model after formula entries

Prior to examining how we can track changes in our portfolio over time, let us establish which parts of this model could also be used in the tracking report model. Clearly the stock name in column A and the cost per share in column D will be important to us in the tracking model. The current market price in column E could also be used.

We may be able to use the information in these parts of the model in our tracking report, and 1-2-3 has the ability to allow us to extract information from other worksheets. By using the /Range,Name command, we can name specific parts of this worksheet, and then call them in to a new worksheet by their range names. Therefore, let us name the three ranges with the commands as follows:

/Range,Name,Create,**SNAME**↲,**A5.A14**↲
/Range,Name,Create,**COST**↲,**D5.D14**↲
/Range,Name,Create,**PRICE**↲,**E5.E14**↲

Having named these data areas so that they may be later recalled, we may save our model with the /**FS** command by entering:

/File,Save,**B:STOCK**↲

to save our model under the name STOCK on the diskette in drive B.

The Tracking Report

Suppose we wish to track the value of our portfolio over a period of time. To accomplish this, we will first create a new model containing only the stock name and cost per share. Thus, let us use the /**WE** command to clear our spreadsheet.

Let us assume we want to place the security names in column A and security prices for each particular tracking period in columns B, C, D, etc. Thus, we should set the format of column A to a width of 15 positions and columns B and beyond to display data with 3 decimal points to accurately reflect the manner in which security prices vary by eighths.

To set the width of column A to 15 positions we would move the active cell to any cell in column A and enter the command:

/**W**orksheet,**C**olumn-Width,**S**et,**15**↲

To set columns B and beyond to display 3 decimal digits, we will use the /**R**ange,**F**ormat,**F**ixed command. Assuming we wish to include five price dates in our tracking, we would enter the command:

/Range,Format,Fixed,**3**↲,**B1.F20**↲

Now that our column formats are established we can use the /**FCCN** command to selectively load columns A and D from our previous model into columns A and B in our newly created model. This is accomplished by the following /**FCCN** commands.

First place the active cell in cell A5 and issue the command:

/File,Combine,Copy,Named Range,**SNAME⤶,B:STOCK⤶**

This copies the stock names into cells A5 through A14.

Then move the active cell to cell B5 and issue the command:

/File,Combine,Copy,Named Range,**COST⤶,B:STOCK⤶**

This copies the cost per share column of figures from the saved model into cells B5 through B14.

Then move the active cell to cell C5 and issue the command:

/File,Combine,Copy,Named Range,**PRICE⤶,B:STOCK⤶**

to place the current prices into cells C5 through C14.

As a result of the three preceding /**FCCN** commands, our model would appear like figure 21.4, with the appropriate heading added in rows 1 through 4.

```
A1: '                                                         READY


           A           B         C         D      E        F       G
 1                     SECURITY PRICE TRACKING REPORT
 2
 3    STOCK-NAME       1/31/8X   2/28/8X
 4    ----------------------------------------------------------------
 5    Abbet Corp.      52.375    54.000
 6    Barber Inc.      23.750    26.500
 7    Carlton Mfg.     17.250    30.875
 8    Davidson Inc.    16.750    17.500
 9    Diskco Corp.      8.250     8.000
10    Dummy Motors     27.500    19.875
11    General Brick     5.875     4.750
12    Tbird Roofing    12.625    14.000
13    Zebra Motors     18.375    18.375
14    Zulta Electric   22.500    21.750
15
16
17
18
19
20
```

Figure 21.4. Track model

Let us save this model under the filename SECTRACK for security tracking by entering the command:

/File,Save,**B:SECTRACK**⏎

Now let us assume that we just updated our portfolio and resaved our model under the filename STOCK. If we wish to add the new security prices to our security tracking model we would clear our spreadsheet and load the file SECTRACK. Then we would load the relevant portion of column E from the file STOCK, this time using cell D5 as the upper left cell value for the area into which the loading process commences.

Suppose we have updated our portfolio four times, resulting in the SECTRACK file containing five security values. This model with appropriate headings might appear like figure 21.5.

A1: '   READY

```
              A          B         C         D        E        F        G
 1                    SECURITY PRICE TRACKING REPORT
 2
 3    STOCK-NAME      1/31/8X   2/28/8X   3/31/8X  4/30/8X  5/31/8X
 4    ------------------------------------------------------------------------
 5    Abbet Corp.      52.375    54.000    54.500   55.750   58.875
 6    Barber Inc.      23.750    26.500    24.625   25.000   26.250
 7    Carlton Mfg.     17.250    30.875    27.125   27.250   27.000
 8    Davidson Inc.    16.750    17.500    15.875   16.125   16.125
 9    Diskco Corp.      8.250     8.000     8.000    8.000    8.250
10    Dummy Motors     27.500    19.875    21.750   22.000   23.875
11    General Brick     5.875     4.750     5.375    5.500    5.375
12    Tbird Roofing    12.625    14.000    13.000   14.500   15.000
13    Zebra Motors     18.375    18.375    19.000   19.375   20.125
14    Zulta Electric   22.500    21.750    22.000   22.250   22.125
15
16
17
18
19
20
```

Figure 21.5. Tracking model after updates

Plotting Our Security Values

Now that we have five prices for each of our securities, we could plot their prices over time to obtain a visual representation of their price fluctuation. To accomplish this, we will use the /G command to plot a line graph of the price of four of the securities over the five time periods.

We will tell 1-2-3 that we wish to plot a line graph and set the X range by entering the command:

/Graph,Type,Line,**X,B3.F3**⏎

Since we wish titles for each axis and a title for the graph itself, we continue the /G command by entering:

Options,Titles,**X**-Axis,**PERIOD ENDING**⏎,Titles,**Y**-Axis,

PRICE⏎,Titles,First,**SECURITY PRICE TRACKING REPORT**⏎,**Q**uit

Next we will assign data variable ranges for the four securities we wish to plot on the graph. Thus, we continue the /G command by entering:

A,B5.F5⏎,**B,B6.F6**⏎,**C,B7.F7**⏎,**D,B8.F8**⏎

Finally, we wish to have a legend designating each of the securities being plotted by name, so we enter:

Options,Legend,**A,ABBET**⏎,Legend,**B,BARBER**⏎,

Legend,**C,CARLTON**⏎,Legend,**D,DAVIDSON**⏎,**Q**uit

Now that we have defined the graph we want 1-2-3 to create for us, we can look at it on the screen, assuming that we have graphics capabilities by entering the command:

View

1-2-3 will draw the line graph of our four securities on the screen so that we may examine it. To return to our model, we may simply press any key on the keyboard. We may now save our graph for later printing and return to our model by entering:

Save,**B:GRAFTAC**⏎,**Q**uit

In order to print our graph, we must exit the spreadsheet part of the LOTUS 1-2-3 system and use the PrintGraph utility provided as part of this powerful integrated package. Prior to leaving our model, we should again save it with the command:

/File,Save,B:SECTRACK⏎

Then, we exit the spreadsheet with the command:

/Quit,**Y**es

To use the PrintGraph utility and select a graph for printing we enter the command:

PrintGraph,**S**elect

We then use the cursor keys on the numeric keypad to move the highlighted area of the screen to the name GRAFTRAK. Next, press the space bar and notice the pound sign (#) appear on the left of the name GRAF-TRAK. This causes the graph to be selected for printing. Press the ⏎ key, then enter the command:

Options,**F**onts,**1**

Again use the cursor keys to move the highlighted area to the name BLOCK1 and press the space bar to select this print font, then press the ⏎ key and enter **Q**uit to exit the Option selections. We may now print our graph with the command **G**o, force the printer to the top of a new page after printing with the **P**age command, and exit the PrintGraph utility with the command:

Quit,**Y**es

The results of our printing the graph are illustrated in figure 21.6.

It should be noted that we can enter the /G commands in any order we desire, however, since the graphing process can take several minutes, it is a good idea for one to double check all assignments prior to executing the graphing process.

Modifications to Consider

The reader should be able to modify the models developed in this chapter to fit his or her particular requirements. Some readers may wish to add a column to include the purchase date of the security as well as a sell date to maintain a historical record of transactions. Since a sold security should no longer be included in our portfolio computations, we could then modify our formulas to reflect the status of the security. To accomplish this we could use the IF function with the following format:

@IF(expression 1, value 2, value 3)

When expression 1 is true, value 2 is entered into the cell containing the IF function while a condition resulting in expression 1 being false causes value 3 to be entered into the cell. Assuming we inserted two

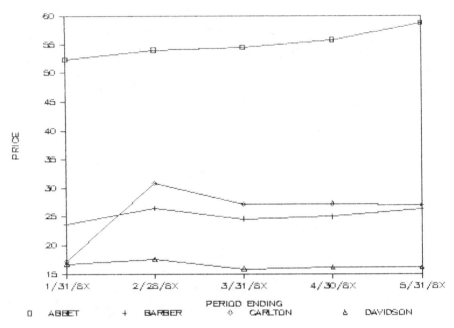

Figure 21.6. Tracking report graph

columns into the STOCK model to contain the dates when the security was sold and the selling price per share, we could test the values of the column containing the selling price in an IF function. To see this, let us assume we modified our model, inserting new columns D and E for the selling date and selling price. Then the market value would appear in column I and its value would be based upon the product of the number of shares and the market price which would be contained in columns B and G. Thus, we would enter the formula @IF(E5>0, 0, +B5*G5) into cell I5 and copy this formula throughout column I. Here the IF expression would set the market value to zero if a selling price for a stock was entered into column E, assuming we sold the stock for more than zero and it did not become worthless. If the stock was not sold, the market value would be entered as the product of cells B5 and G5. Similarly, we could change the formulas for annual income and current yield and we could add additional columns to include a purchase date and other information in our model.

22

Taxable Versus Tax Free
Security Analysis

Concept

To escape the long arm of the Internal Revenue Service, many
investors have purchased a variety of municipal bonds whose interest
payments are exempt from Federal Income Tax. In addition to considering the merits of the issuer of the bond, investors must compare the yield
offered by this type of security to the yield offered by taxable securities.
Doing so permits the investor to determine which category of security
offers a higher return for his or her investment.

Since the after tax yield of a taxable security depends upon the
investor's federal, state and local tax brackets, we must determine or

estimate our marginal tax rate for these three tax categories. By marginal tax rate we mean the percent of each additional dollar of income that will be taxed by each taxing authority. The formula to compute the after tax yield of a taxable security is:

$$\text{After Tax Yield} = \text{Taxable Yield} * (1-(F+F*(S+L)))$$

where:

F = marginal federal tax rate
S = marginal state tax rate
L = marginal local tax rate

As an example, consider a corporate bond that pays 15% interest. Assume we are in the 50% federal tax bracket and 6% state tax bracket and do not pay local taxes. Our after tax yield is computed as follows:

$$\text{After Tax Yield} = .15*(1-(.50+.50*.06)) = .0705$$

From the preceding, we should be indifferent to the purchase of a taxable security yielding 15% and a security that is exempt from federal and state taxes that yields 7.05%, assuming both securities have equivalent ratings.

If we are offered a tax free security by our broker we will want to determine its taxable equivalent yield based upon our marginal tax brackets. The formula to compute the taxable equivalent yield given the tax free yield of a security is:

$$\text{Taxable Equivalent Yield} = \frac{\text{Tax Free Yield}}{(1-(F+F*(S+L)))}$$

where F, S and L represent one's federal, state and local marginal tax brackets. As an example of the use of this formula, let us examine a security that is free of federal and state taxes. If the security is priced to yield 7.05% and we are in the 50% federal tax bracket and 6% state tax bracket, what yield would a taxable security have to offer to equal the tax free yield of this security? Substitution into the previously defined formula results in the following:

$$\text{Taxable Equivalent Yield} = \frac{\text{Tax Free Yield}}{(1-(F+F^*(S+L)))}$$

$$\text{Taxable Equivalent Yield} = \frac{.0705}{1-(.5+(.06))} = \frac{.0705}{.47} = .15$$

Thus, as we should expect from our first example, a tax free yield of 7.05% is equivalent to a taxable yield of 15% based upon the assumed federal and state marginal tax rates used in the example.

Constructing the Model

Although we could use the previously presented formulas and a calculator to perform our taxable and tax free equivalent yield computations, it is often desirable to obtain tables of such computations. Since many securities are offered to the public on a daily basis such tables simplify our decision criteria to a table lookup process.

For each model we will use the variables F, S and L to represent one's federal, state and local tax brackets. Although we will initialize these variables to .5, .06 and 0, one can easily change these values to correspond to one's actual tax brackets.

The model we will construct will produce a table to tax free equivalent yields based upon a varying taxable yield. Although security prices normally vary by one-eighth of a percent, we will initialize a taxable yield value and then vary that amount by one-quarter of one percent throughout the range we desire to assign to our model to reduce the size of our table for illustrative purposes. Figure 22.1 shows the headings we could enter into our model that will result in the computation of a column of tax free yields based upon one's federal, state and local tax brackets and a given taxable yield. Note that one's federal, state and local tax brackets expressed as a percent will be entered into cells C5, E5 and G5 respectively. Also note that we have entered the first value for the taxable yield column (.08) into cell C9 and the formula to compute the equivalent tax free yield into cell E9. Here the tax free yield is expressed in terms of the taxable yield (cell C9) and the federal (cell C5), state (cell E5) and local (cell G5) marginal tax brackets based upon the formula previously presented in this chapter. We have also turned on the formula display by entering the command:

/Worksheet,Global,Format,Text

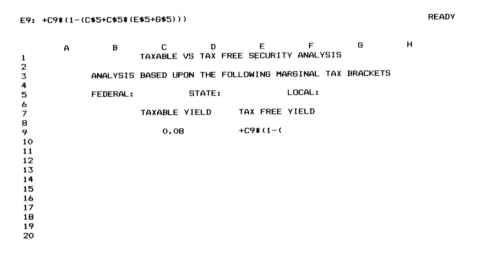

Figure 22.1. Model headings

Assuming we wish to construct our table based upon a range of taxable yields varying from 8% to 11% in increments of one-quarter of one percent, 13 entries will be required in column C, beginning in row 9 and incrementing by .0025 through row 21 in column A. To obtain the desired sequence, we can position the active cell at C10 and enter the formula +C9+.0025. Next, we can use the /C command to copy this formula through cell C21 as follows:

/Copy,C10↵,C11.C21↵

Once we enter the copy command the contents of the cells in column C will appear as follows:

```
C7:  'TAXABLE YIELD
C9:  (F6) 0.08
C10: (F6) +C9+0.0025
C11: (F6) +C10+0.0025
C12: (F6) +C11+0.0025
C13: (F6) +C12+0.0025
C14: (F6) +C13+0.0025
C15: (F6) +C14+0.0025
C16: (F6) +C15+0.0025
C17: (F6) +C16+0.0025
C18: (F6) +C17+0.0025
C19: (F6) +C18+0.0025
C20: (F6) +C19+0.0025
C21: (F6) +C20+0.0025
```

Now let us focus our attention upon the tax free yield column. Since we wish to compute the tax free yield that is equivalent to the taxable yields entered in column C, we will again use the /C command when we copy the formula in cell E9 to cells E10 through E21 with the following command:

/Copy,E9-⌐,E10.E21-⌐

Note that the values for C5, E5, and G5 are not changed in the copied formulas because we used the dollar sign ($) to designate to 1-2-3 that they are references to an absolute cell in the spreadsheet. After the copy is completed, the contents of column E from cells E7 through E21 would appear as follows:

```
E7:  'TAX FREE YIELD
E9:  (F6)  +C9*(1-(C$5+C$5*(E$5+G$5)))
E10: (F6)  +C10*(1-(C$5+C$5*(E$5+G$5)))
E11: (F6)  +C11*(1-(C$5+C$5*(E$5+G$5)))
E12: (F6)  +C12*(1-(C$5+C$5*(E$5+G$5)))
E13: (F6)  +C13*(1-(C$5+C$5*(E$5+G$5)))
E14: (F6)  +C14*(1-(C$5+C$5*(E$5+G$5)))
E15: (F6)  +C15*(1-(C$5+C$5*(E$5+G$5)))
E16: (F6)  +C16*(1-(C$5+C$5*(E$5+G$5)))
E17: (F6)  +C17*(1-(C$5+C$5*(E$5+G$5)))
E18: (F6)  +C18*(1-(C$5+C$5*(E$5+G$5)))
E19: (F6)  +C19*(1-(C$5+C$5*(E$5+G$5)))
E20: (F6)  +C20*(1-(C$5+C$5*(E$5+G$5)))
E21: (F6)  +C21*(1-(C$5+C$5*(E$5+G$5)))
```

By entering the values for federal, state and local marginal tax brackets previously discussed into cells C5, E5 and G5 and entering the command:

/Worksheet,Global,Format,General

our screen should appear as shown in figure 22.2.

```
A1:                                                                  READY

         A      B        C       D       E       F       G       H
1                     TAXABLE VS TAX FREE SECURITY ANALYSIS
2
3             ANALYSIS BASED UPON THE FOLLOWING MARGINAL TAX BRACKETS
4
5             FEDERAL:   0.5 STATE:      0.06 LOCAL:          0
6
7                     TAXABLE YIELD      TAX FREE YIELD
8
9                        0.08               0.0376
10                       0.0825             0.038775
11                       0.085              0.03995
12                       0.0875             0.041125
13                       0.09               0.0423
14                       0.0925             0.043475
15                       0.095              0.04465
16                       0.0975             0.045825
17                       0.1                0.047
18                       0.1025             0.048175
19                       0.105              0.04935
20                       0.1075             0.050525
```

Figure 22.2. Model after entry of values and formulas

We can enter the command:

/Range,Format,Fixed,6↵,C9.E21↵

to align our decimal points and make our model easier to read. This would result in the following screen appearing like figure 22.3.

```
A1:                                                                    READY


     A        B          C         D          E          F        G        H
1                        TAXABLE VS TAX FREE SECURITY ANALYSIS
2
3              ANALYSIS BASED UPON THE FOLLOWING MARGINAL TAX BRACKETS
4
5              FEDERAL:      0.5 STATE:        0.06 LOCAL:         0
6
7                        TAXABLE YIELD       TAX FREE YIELD
8
9                        0.080000            0.037600
10                       0.082500            0.038775
11                       0.085000            0.039950
12                       0.087500            0.041125
13                       0.090000            0.042300
14                       0.092500            0.043475
15                       0.095000            0.044650
16                       0.097500            0.045825
17                       0.100000            0.047000
18                       0.102500            0.048175
19                       0.105000            0.049350
20                       0.107500            0.050525
```

Figure 22.3. Model with border removed and columns left justified

From the preceding table, we would require a tax free yield of at least 5.0525% if taxable yields were 10.75% based upon a marginal federal tax bracket of 50% and a marginal state tax bracket of 6%. If our broker offered us a tax free security yielding less than 5.0525% and a taxable security yielding 10.75%, we should purchase the taxable security. Similarly, if our broker offered us a tax free security yielding more than 5.0525% and a taxable security yielding 10.75%, we should purchase the tax free security.

Prior to leaving this model, we may wish to save it to disk as this would facilitate modifying it at a later date. The command:

/File,Save,B:TAXFREE↵

would save our model under the name TAXFREE on the diskette in drive B. Now suppose we are anticipating moving to a city in a state with a high income tax as well as a local tax. To determine the effect of a change in state and local marginal tax rates upon the tax free yield we can use the /FR command to retrieve the file previously saved and modify the relevant data cells. If we estimate our marginal state tax bracket will be 14% and the local tax bracket 8%, we can enter these changes into cells E5 and G5 and 1-2-3 will automatically recalculate our table of tax free yields with the results shown in figure 22.4.

```
G5: 0.08                                                          READY

      A      B         C       D       E        F        G        H
1                    TAXABLE VS TAX FREE SECURITY ANALYSIS
2
3            ANALYSIS BASED UPON THE FOLLOWING MARGINAL TAX BRACKETS
4
5            FEDERAL:     0.5 STATE:      0.14 LOCAL:      0.08
6
7                     TAXABLE YIELD      TAX FREE YIELD
8
9                       0.080000          0.031200
10                      0.082500          0.032175
11                      0.085000          0.033150
12                      0.087500          0.034125
13                      0.090000          0.035100
14                      0.092500          0.036075
15                      0.095000          0.037050
16                      0.097500          0.038025
17                      0.100000          0.039000
18                      0.102500          0.039975
19                      0.105000          0.040950
20                      0.107500          0.041925
```

Figure 22.4. Model after recalculation

A Variation to Consider

A second model one may wish to construct would use a range of tax free yields to compute the equivalent taxable equivalent yields. Here, one would use the formula:

$$\text{Taxable Equivalent Yield} = \frac{\text{Tax Free Yield}}{(1-(F+F^*(S+L)))}$$

where F, S and L represent one's federal, state and local marginal tax brackets. The column on the left of our model would contain the desired range of tax free yields while the column on the right would contain the formula that would result in the computation of the equivalent taxable yield. The construction of this variation of our taxable versus tax free security analysis model is left to the reader as an exercise.

23

Warrant Analysis

Concept

A warrant is an option to purchase a stated number of shares of a stock at a specified price. For example, XYZ Corporation may have a warrant outstanding that provides the warrant holder with the right to purchase one share of the company's stock at a price of $20 for each warrant held.

Although warrants normally expire on a certain date, some warrants may be extended by the company while others may be issued with perpetual lives. Since a warrant has no value after its expiration, one should carefully check its expiration date prior to purchase.

Warrants have both a calculated or formula value and an actual value or price that is determined by market conditions. The formula value of a warrant is computed as follows:

Formula Value = (Stock Price - Option Price) x Conversion Rate

where:

Stock Price	- is the market price of the common stock one receives upon exercising the warrant.
Option Price	- is the price one pays for the common stock if he or she holds a warrant to be exercised.
Conversion Rate	- is the number of shares of common stock the warrant holder is entitled to purchase for each warrant held.

Suppose the previously mentioned XYZ Corporation warrant's option price is $30, the conversion rate is 1.0 shares of common stock currently sells for $50 per share. The formula value of the warrant is:

Formula Value = (50-30)*1.0 = $20

if the warrant is selling for $25, its premium is:

Premium = (Warrant Price - Formula Value) = ($25-$20) = $5

A warrant normally sells in excess of its formula value due to the leverage it provides the investor in comparison to purchasing common stock. For example, by purchasing a warrant for $25 one in effect controls one share of common stock which would otherwise cost $50 to purchase. By purchasing two warrants at $25 apiece, one in effect controls two shares of common stock for the price of one share. In this example, the leverage ratio is:

$$\text{Leverage Ratio} = \frac{\text{Stock Price}}{\text{Warrant Price}} = \frac{50}{25} = 2.0$$

A few additional items require discussion concerning warrants. First, when the stock is selling for less than the warrant's option price, the formula value of the warrant is negative. In actuality, the warrant price will always be greater than zero until it expires. Thus, since a formula value less than zero makes no sense, one could define the formula value to be zero when the stock price is selling for less than the option price. Secondly, as a stock rises in price the premium of the warrant over its formula value will normally decline. This is due both to the loss of leverage as well as a loss in the amount of protection one gains from normally purchasing a warrant. For example, if the common stock rises in price to $100 the formula value of the warrant would become ($100-$30)*1.0 or $70. Not considering any premium for the warrant, its leverage ratio would be 100/70 or 1.42. Similarly, one's downside protection diminishes if the stock price should fall in value. If the stock price fell in half from $100 to $50 per share, the formula value of the warrant would decrease from $70 to $20, a loss of $50. If the stock were selling at $50 per share the warrant's formula value would be $20, representing a 60 percent reduction in the warrant's value when the common stock declined by 50 percent.

Constructing the Model

Although we cannot construct a model that will calculate the actual value of a warrant since its price is controlled by market conditions, we can examine the potential effect of the movement in the price of a stock upon the warrant's formula value and leverage ratio. The following model provides us with an analysis of the changes in the warrant's formula value and leverage ratio based upon a ±50% change in the price of common stock which the warrant converts into. To use this model one only has to enter the option price, warrant price, conversion rate and stock price at the appropriate locations in a column of the model.

Let us put the heading of our model in cell D1 and the labels for the OPTION PRICE, WARRANT PRICE, CONVERSION RATE and STOCK PRICE in cells A3 through A6. Since we wish to initially compute the FORMULA, LEVERAGE RATIO, PREMIUM (DOLLARS) and PREMIUM (PERCENT), let us enter these labels as text into cells E3 through E6. Next we will enter the heading POTENTIAL

STOCK MOVEMENT ANALYSIS into cell C8. As we wish to explore
the effect of potential stock movement upon the warrant we will also enter
the headings STOCK MOVEMENT into cell B10 and WARRANT
EFFECT into cell E10.

We will have two columns of calculations to be performed under
STOCK MOVEMENT to examine the variance in stock price and its
percent change. Thus, we can enter the label STOCK PRICE into cell
A11 and % CHANGE into cell C11. Under the WARRANT EFFECT
heading we will wish to examine the change in the formula value, leverage
ratio and the percent change in the formula value. Thus, we can enter the
labels FORMULA VALUE, LEVERAGE RATIO and % CHANGE in
cells D11, F11 and H11 respectively. Based upon the preceding, our initial
model consisting only of labels entered as text would appear as shown in
figure 23.1.

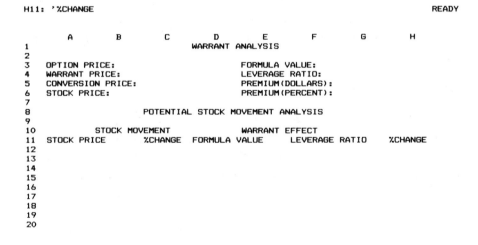

Figure 23.1. Model with labels

Now we are ready to enter the appropriate formulas to compute the
formula value, leverage ratio and the premium of the warrant's price over
its formula value both in dollars and as a percent.

Since we will enter the four required data elements into cells C3 through C6, we will reference these cells for our computations. Thus, the formula value becomes (C6-C3)*C5 which is entered into cell G3. The leverage ratio is obtained by dividing the stock price by the warrant price so we will enter the formula +C6/C4 into cell G4. Next, the premium in dollars is simply the warrant price minus the formula value which was computed in cell G3. Thus, we will enter the formula +C4-G3 into cell G5. The premium of the warrant as a percent of its formula value is obtained by first subtracting its formula value from the warrant price. Then we would divide the result by the formula value and multiply the result of the division by 100. Thus, we would enter the formula ((C4-G3)/G3)*100 into cell G6.

To see the formulas enter into the preceding cells, we can use the /WGF command as follows:

/Worksheet,Global,Format,Text

and to see all of the formula in column G, we enter:

/Worksheet,Column-Width,Set,17⏎

If we have entered our formulas correctly, the model should appear as shown in figure 23.2.

```
G6: ((C4-G3)/G3)*100                                          READY


         A         B         C         D         E       F         G
1                                       WARRANT ANALYSIS
2
3    OPTION PRICE:                          FORMULA VALUE:       (C6-C3)*C5
4    WARRANT PRICE:                         LEVERAGE RATIO:      +C6/C4
5    CONVERSION PRICE:                      PREMIUM(DOLLARS):    +C4-G3
6    STOCK PRICE:                           PREMIUM(PERCENT):    ((C4-G3)/G3)*100
7
8                        POTENTIAL STOCK MOVEMENT ANALYSIS
9
10              STOCK MOVEMENT                WARRANT EFFECT
11   STOCK PRICE        %CHANGE   FORMULA VALUE      LEVERAGE RATIO
12
13
14
15
16
17
18
19
20
```

Figure 23.2. Model with formula entries displayed

Now we are ready to enter the appropriate formulas under each of the five column headings in row 11. If we assume that we wish to examine the effect of a ±50% change in the price of the stock upon the warrant, we can obtain this variance in stock price by entering .5*C6 in cell A12, .6*C6 in cell A13 and so on, until 1.5*C6 is entered into cell A22. After completing the entry of these formulas, we find our model would appear as shown in figure 23.3.

A22: 1.5*C6   READY

```
          A       B          C         D        E           F              G
3     OPTION PRICE:                              FORMULA VALUE:       (C6-C3)*C5
4     WARRANT PRICE:                             LEVERAGE RATIO:      +C6/C4
5     CONVERSION PRICE:                          PREMIUM(DOLLARS):    +C4-G3
6     STOCK PRICE:                               PREMIUM(PERCENT):    ((C4-G3)/G3)*100
7
8                        POTENTIAL STOCK MOVEMENT ANALYSIS
9
10              STOCK MOVEMENT              WARRANT EFFECT
11    STOCK PRICE         %CHANGE   FORMULA VALUE     LEVERAGE RATIO
12    0.5*C6
13    0.6*C6
14    0.7*C6
15    0.8*C6
16    0.9*C6
17    1*C6
18    1.1*C6
19    1.2*C6
20    1.3*C6
21    1.4*C6
22    1.5*C6
```

Figure 23.3. Model after entry of formulas in column A

Now let us focus our attention upon the % CHANGE column under cell C11. The percent change in the stock price is computed by first subtracting the stock price to be entered in cell C6 from the computed stock price in cells A12 through A22. Next we would divide the result by the stock price entered in cell C6 and multiply the result of that computation by 100. Thus, the formula we would enter into cell C12 would be:

((A12-C$6)/C$6)*100

Since a similar formula is required to be entered into cells C13 through C22 we can use the /C command to copy the formula entered into cell C12. Based upon the preceding, our /C command would become:

/Copy,C12⏎,C13.C22⏎

After the copy operation is completed, the contents of cells C11 through C22 would be as follows:

```
C11:  (F2)  '%CHANGE
C12:  (F2)  ((A12-C$6)/C$6)*100
C13:  (F2)  ((A13-C$6)/C$6)*100
C14:  (F2)  ((A14-C$6)/C$6)*100
C15:  (F2)  ((A15-C$6)/C$6)*100
C16:  (F2)  ((A16-C$6)/C$6)*100
C17:  (F2)  ((A17-C$6)/C$6)*100
C18:  (F2)  ((A18-C$6)/C$6)*100
C19:  (F2)  ((A19-C$6)/C$6)*100
C20:  (F2)  ((A20-C$6)/C$6)*100
C21:  (F2)  ((A21-C$6)/C$6)*100
C22:  (F2)  ((A22-C$6)/C$6)*100
```

Now let us focus our attention upon the formula value computations required to be entered in cells D12 through D22. Since the formula value is computed by determining the difference between the stock price and option price and multiplying this amount by the conversion rate, our entry into cell D12 would be the formula:

(A12-C$3)*C$5

As we wish to examine the effect of varying the stock price upon the warrant's formula value, only the value of A12 will change as we copy the formula previously entered into cell D12 from cell D13 through cell D22. Thus, we would enter the following /C command:

/Copy,D12⏎,D13.D22⏎

After this copy operation is completed, the contents of cells D11 through D22 would be as follows:

```
D11:  (F2)  'FORMULA VALUE
D12:  (F2)  (A12-C$3)*C$5
D13:  (F2)  (A13-C$3)*C$5
D14:  (F2)  (A14-C$3)*C$5
D15:  (F2)  (A15-C$3)*C$5
D16:  (F2)  (A16-C$3)*C$5
D17:  (F2)  (A17-C$3)*C$5
D18:  (F2)  (A18-C$3)*C$5
D19:  (F2)  (A19-C$3)*C$5
D20:  (F2)  (A20-C$3)*C$5
D21:  (F2)  (A21-C$3)*C$5
D22:  (F2)  (A22-C$3)*C$5
```

Now let us focus our attention upon the column of leverage ratio calculations required to be entered into our model from cell F12 through cell F22. The leverage ratio was previously defined as the stock price divided by the warrant price so we would enter +A12/C$4 into cell F12. Next we will use the /C command to copy the formula entered in cell F12 through cells F13 to F22 as follows:

/Copy,F12⏎,F13.F22⏎

As a result of our copy operation the contents of cells F11 through F22 would become:

```
F11:  (F2)  'LEVERAGE RATIO
F12:  (F2)  +A12/C$4
F13:  (F2)  +A13/C$4
F14:  (F2)  +A14/C$4
F15:  (F2)  +A15/C$4
F16:  (F2)  +A16/C$4
F17:  (F2)  +A17/C$4
F18:  (F2)  +A18/C$4
F19:  (F2)  +A19/C$4
F20:  (F2)  +A20/C$4
F21:  (F2)  +A21/C$4
F22:  (F2)  +A22/C$4
```

The last set of calculations required for our model will begin in cell H12. Here we wish to compute the percent change between the formula value previously calculated in Column D and the original formula value which was computed in cell G3. Thus, our first entry into cell H12 would be:

$$((D12-G\$3)/G\$3)*100$$

Once again, we can use the /C command to copy this formula. Here, our /C command would be:

/Copy,H12┘,H13.H22┘

After this copy is completed, the contents of cells H11 through H22 would be:

```
H11:  (F2)  '%CHANGE
H12:  (F2)  ((D12-G$3)/G$3)*100
H13:  (F2)  ((D13-G$3)/G$3)*100
H14:  (F2)  ((D14-G$3)/G$3)*100
H15:  (F2)  ((D15-G$3)/G$3)*100
H16:  (F2)  ((D16-G$3)/G$3)*100
H17:  (F2)  ((D17-G$3)/G$3)*100
H18:  (F2)  ((D18-G$3)/G$3)*100
H19:  (F2)  ((D19-G$3)/G$3)*100
H20:  (F2)  ((D20-G$3)/G$3)*100
H21:  (F2)  ((D21-G$3)/G$3)*100
H22:  (F2)  ((D22-G$3)/G$3)*100
```

DATA ENTRY

Now that we have completed entering our formulas, we will probably use the /WGFG command to turn our formula display off and the /WCS9┘ to reset column G to 9 positions in preparation for entering data. After entering the command:

/Worksheet,Global,Format,General

to turn the formula display off, we will most likely assume we made several errors due to the display of ERR in many cells of our model. Unless we entered our formulas incorrectly we can disregard these error messages as they refer to cells where a division by zero is occurring. Since we have yet to enter any data, the contents of cells C3 through C6 are zero and any references to these cells in the denominator of a formula will cause the message ERR to be displayed in a cell containing this type of formula.

Let us move to cell C3 and enter the option price as 30. Similarly, let us enter 25 for the warrant price, 1 for the conversion ratio and 50 for the stock price into cells C4 through C6. Note the resulting computations remove the ERR indicators since the denominators in the formulas now are assigned values based upon the data we entered into cells C3 through C6.

For a more professional looking display, let us use the /WGFF command to display numeric values with 2 decimal points by entering:

/Worksheet,Global,Format,Fixed,2┘

Our warrant analysis model using the sample data previously entered would appear as shown in figure 23.4.

```
A1:  (F2)                                                              READY

          A        B        C        D        E       F        G        H
 1                               WARRANT ANALYSIS
 2
 3    OPTION PRICE:        30.00          FORMULA VALUE:      20.00
 4    WARRANT PRICE:       25.00          LEVERAGE RATIO:      2.00
 5    CONVERSION PRICE:     1.00          PREMIUM(DOLLARS):    5.00
 6    STOCK PRICE:         50.00          PREMIUM(PERCENT):   25.00
 7
 8                         POTENTIAL STOCK MOVEMENT ANALYSIS
 9
10              STOCK MOVEMENT              WARRANT EFFECT
11    STOCK PRICE      %CHANGE   FORMULA VALUE   LEVERAGE RATIO    %CHANGE
12      25.00          -50.00      -5.00             1.00         -125.00
13      30.00          -40.00       0.00             1.20         -100.00
14      35.00          -30.00       5.00             1.40          -75.00
15      40.00          -20.00      10.00             1.60          -50.00
16      45.00          -10.00      15.00             1.80          -25.00
17      50.00            0.00      20.00             2.00            0.00
18      55.00           10.00      25.00             2.20           25.00
19      60.00           20.00      30.00             2.40           50.00
20      65.00           30.00      35.00             2.60           75.00
```

Figure 23.4.   Model with sample data

Now that the model is completed, we can change the entries in cells C3 through C6 to specific values that reflect warrants we wish to analyze. Note that each time we change the entries in cells C3 through C6, 59 computations will automatically occur based upon the formulas entered into our model, once again illustrating the versatility of constructing a basic spreadsheet model and exercising the model as required.

CELL CONTENTS

To facilitate the reconstruction of this model, we will conclude this chapter with a listing of the cell contents of the model previously developed. It should be noted that cells C3 through C6 are the only cells required to be modified by the reader as these are the cells into which the four data values relevant to one's warrant analysis are to be entered.

```
D1:   (F2)   'WARRANT ANALYSIS
A3:   (F2)   'OPTION PRICE:
C3:   (F2)   30
E3:   (F2)   'FORMULA VALUE:
G3:   (F2)   (C6-C3)*C5
A4:   (F2)   'WARRANT PRICE:
C4:   (F2)   25
E4:   (F2)   'LEVERAGE RATIO:
G4:   (F2)   +C6/C4
A5:   (F2)   'CONVERSION PRICE:
C5:   (F2)   1
E5:   (F2)   'PREMIUM(DOLLARS):
G5:   (F2)   +C4-G3
A6:   (F2)   'STOCK PRICE:
C6:   (F2)   50
E6:   (F2)   'PREMIUM(PERCENT):
G6:   (F2)   ((C4-G3)/G3)*100
C8:   (F2)   'POTENTIAL STOCK MOVEMENT ANALYSIS
B10:  (F2)   'STOCK MOVEMENT
E10:  (F2)   'WARRANT EFFECT
A11:  (F2)   'STOCK PRICE
C11:  (F2)   '%CHANGE
D11:  (F2)   'FORMULA VALUE
F11:  (F2)   'LEVERAGE RATIO
```

continued on following page

```
H11:    (F2)    '%CHANGE
A12:    (F2)    0.5*C6
C12:    (F2)    ((A12-C$6)/C$6)*100
D12:    (F2)    (A12-C$3)*C$5
F12:    (F2)    +A12/C$4
H12:    (F2)    ((D12-G$3)/G$3)*100
A13:    (F2)    0.6*C6
C13:    (F2)    ((A13-C$6)/C$6)*100
D13:    (F2)    (A13-C$3)*C$5
F13:    (F2)    +A13/C$4
H13:    (F2)    ((D13-G$3)/G$3)*100
A14:    (F2)    0.7*C6
C14:    (F2)    ((A14-C$6)/C$6)*100
D14:    (F2)    (A14-C$3)*C$5
F14:    (F2)    +A14/C$4
H14:    (F2)    ((D14-G$3)/G$3)*100
A15:    (F2)    0.8*C6
C15:    (F2)    ((A15-C$6)/C$6)*100
D15:    (F2)    (A15-C$3)*C$5
F15:    (F2)    +A15/C$4
H15:    (F2)    ((D15-G$3)/G$3)*100
A16:    (F2)    0.9*C6
C16:    (F2)    ((A16-C$6)/C$6)*100
D16:    (F2)    (A16-C$3)*C$5
F16:    (F2)    +A16/C$4
H16:    (F2)    ((D16-G$3)/G$3)*100
A17:    (F2)    1*C6
C17:    (F2)    ((A17-C$6)/C$6)*100
D17:    (F2)    (A17-C$3)*C$5
F17:    (F2)    +A17/C$4
H17:    (F2)    ((D17-G$3)/G$3)*100
A18:    (F2)    1.1*C6
C18:    (F2)    ((A18-C$6)/C$6)*100
D18:    (F2)    (A18-C$3)*C$5
F18:    (F2)    +A18/C$4
H18:    (F2)    ((D18-G$3)/G$3)*100
A19:    (F2)    1.2*C6
C19:    (F2)    ((A19-C$6)/C$6)*100
D19:    (F2)    (A19-C$3)*C$5
F19:    (F2)    +A19/C$4
H19:    (F2)    ((D19-G$3)/G$3)*100
```

continued on following page

```
A20:  (F2)  1.3*C6
C20:  (F2)  ((A20-C$6)/C$6)*100
D20:  (F2)  (A20-C$3)*C$5
F20:  (F2)  +A20/C$4
H20:  (F2)  ((D20-G$3)/G$3)*100
A21:  (F2)  1.4*C6
C21:  (F2)  ((A21-C$6)/C$6)*100
D21:  (F2)  (A21-C$3)*C$5
F21:  (F2)  +A21/C$4
H21:  (F2)  ((D21-G$3)/G$3)*100
A22:  (F2)  1.5*C6
C22:  (F2)  ((A22-C$6)/C$6)*100
D22:  (F2)  (A22-C$3)*C$5
F22:  (F2)  +A22/C$4
H22:  (F2)  ((D22-G$3)/G$3)*100
```

24

Entertainment and Programming

Concept

Entertainment is one of America's favorite pastimes, and many people have been using computers for entertainment over the last few years. Few people, however, have considered using a financial spreadsheet such as 1-2-3 for playing games and entertaining themselves. In this chapter we will learn how to use the 1-2-3 random number generator to create a simple game of chance, and show how to program 1-2-3 to control the game.

Constructing the Model

Dice games have always interested man, and craps is one of the most popular games using dice. In craps, one rolls two dice and the game evolves around the random numbers which the dice stop on. 1-2-3 has the ability to produce random numbers with the built in @RAND function, but the random numbers produced are always a decimal fraction. We can easily generate a whole number from a random number by multiplying by 10 and rounding off the number with no decimal places. In 1-2-3, the formula to produce a whole number with no decimal places would be:

@ROUND(@RAND*10,0)

Since we have two dice in a game of craps, we will use this formula twice in our model to generate each of the die values. Let's begin our model by entering the formula @ROUND(@RAND*10,0) into cell B3 to generate a random number for one die. We can copy this formula to cell B4 to generate a second random number for the second die with the command:

/Copy,B3⤶,B4⤶

Now that we have our dice represented in cells B3 and B4, we can sum their total value by entering the formula +B3+B4 into cell B6.

How do we roll the dice again? 1-2-3 has a function key that recalculates the spreadsheet, and this key is the F9 (Calc) key. By simply pressing the F9 key, 1-2-3 will recalculate the spreadsheet and generate new random numbers in cells B3 and B4, thus effectively "rolling the dice" for us. By entering a title of our model and instructions on how to roll the dice, and titles for each die and the total value of the two die, our model will look as follows:

```
B6:  +B3+B4                                                        READY

        A        B          C         D         E        F        G        H
 1   CRAPS GAME - Press the 'F9' key to roll the dice!
 2
 3   DIE #1 =        5
 4   DIE #2 =        2
 5
 6   TOTAL =         7
 7
 8
 9
10
11
12
13
14
15
16
17
18
19
20
```

After rolling the dice a few more times by pressing the F9 key, we may get a model that looks like this:

```
B6:  +B3+B4                                                        READY

        A        B          C         D         E        F        G        H
 1   CRAPS GAME - Press the 'F9' key to roll the dice!
 2
 3   DIE #1 =        9
 4   DIE #2 =        6
 5
 6   TOTAL =        15
 7
 8
 9
10
11
12
13
14
15
16
17
18
19
20
```

Notice that die 1 in this model has a value of 9, but we know that each die can only have the numbers 1 through 6 on them. Therefore we must again roll the dice by pressing F9 until we get two numbers within the range of 1 to 6. This can be very frustrating to us, and 1-2-3 has the capability to control this rolling and checking for valid values on both die for us.

Programming the Roll of the Dice

1-2-3 has a facility that allows us to store sequences of keystrokes for future use. This stored sequence of keystrokes is called a MACRO in 1-2-3 terms. A MACRO can be "attached" to a letter or key on the keyboard, and we can activate the MACRO and execute all the keystrokes stored for use by simply holding down the "Alt" key and typing the letter or key the MACRO is "attached" to. This is a very powerful and useful facility built into 1-2-3 which will allow us to execute many keystrokes at the press of just one key. We will use this MACRO ability of 1-2-3 to control our craps game.

To begin our MACRO, we will enter {CALC}~ into cell D3. The {CALC} part of this command tells 1-2-3 to press the F9 (calc) key, and the tilde (~) character is the symbol for the ⏎ key.

Since we only want our dice to generate the numbers 1 through 6, we can use the /X commands for testing the random numbers generated and rolling again if necessary. Therefore in cell D4 we will enter:

'/XI(B3>0#and#B3<7)#and#(B4>0#and#B4<7)~/XGD6~

in cell D5 enter:

'/XGD3~

in cell D6 enter:

'/XQ

Note that each entry is preceded by a single quote mark (') to tell 1-2-3 that these are label entries and not the start of a 1-2-3 command (which is begun with the '/'). The entry in cell D4 is treated as an "IF" conditional statement and is interpreted as "If the value in cell B3 is in the range 1 through 6, and if the value in cell B4 is in the range 1 through 6, then go to cell D6." The entry in cell D5 is only executed when the "IF" condition in cell D4 is "False". Cell D5 effectively says "Go to cell D3", and cell D6 says "Quit executing this macro".

Thinking through the logic of this MACRO, we can see that we roll the dice in cell D3, test for each die being valid in cell D4, if they are both in the range of 1 to 6 we quit the MACRO in cell D6, and if both die are not in the range of 1 to 6, cell D5 returns control to cell D3 to "roll the dice" again.

Now we need to "attach" our MACRO to a key so that it can be easily executed. We do this with the /RN command as follows:

/Range,Name,Create,\ R↵,D3.D6↵

In the preceding command, the \R attached our MACRO to the letter R on the keyboard so that we could execute our MACRO by holding down the 'Alt' key and pressing the letter 'R'. Let us also move our active cell to any cell in column B and enter the command:

/Worksheet,Column-Width,Set,4↵

This resets the width of column B to 4 character positions and makes our die values much easier to read. Our model now should appear as follows:

```
D6: '/XQ                                                          READY

        A     B      C         D        E        F       G       H
 1   CRAPS GAME - Press the 'F9' key to roll the dice!
 2
 3   DIE #1 =    7         {CALC}~
 4   DIE #2 =    4         /XI(B3)0#and#B3<7)#and#(B4)0#and#B4<7)~/XGD6~
 5                         /XGD3~
 6   TOTAL =    11         /XQ
 7
 8
 9
10
11
12
13
14
15
16
17
18
19
20
```

We only need to change our heading to tell the user how to roll the dice correctly, and now our model appears as follows:

```
A1: 'CRAPS GAME - To roll dice, hold down the 'Alt' key and press 'R' !      READY


      A      B      C       D       E       F       G       H
1   CRAPS GAME - To roll dice, hold down the 'Alt' key and press 'R' !
2
3   DIE #1 =    6          {CALC}~
4   DIE #2 =    5          /XI(B3)0#and#B3<7)#and#(B4)0#and#B4<7)~/XGD6~
5                          /XGD3~
6   TOTAL =    11          /XQ
7
8
9
10
11
12
13
14
15
16
17
18
19
20
```

Now we may roll the dice by simply holding down the 'Alt' key and pressing the letter 'R'. The MACRO will roll the dice over and over until both die have their values in the range 1 to 6. We should now save our model to the diskette in drive B with the command:

/File,Save,B:CRAPS⏎

A listing of the cell formulas is shown below:

```
A1: 'CRAPS GAME - To roll dice, hold down the 'Alt' key and press 'R' !
A3: 'DIE #1 =
B3: @ROUND(@RAND*10,0)
D3: '{CALC}~
A4: 'DIE #2 =
B4: @ROUND(@RAND*10,0)
D4: '/XI(B3)0#and#B3<7)#and#(B4)0#and#B4<7)~/XGD6~
D5: '/XGD3~
A6: 'TOTAL =
B6: +B3+B4
D6: '/XQ
```

While developing this game was relatively simple, one can easily expand on these ideas to create more sophisticated games and entertainment with a spreadsheet.

Index

More Computer Books from Weber Systems Inc.

Apple
Apple Macintosh® Business Software in Basic

IBM
IBM PC AT Networking Strategies (Fall 85)
IBM PC AT User's Handbook
IBM Portable PC® User's Handbook
IBM PCjr® For Students
IBM PC® Business Software in Basic

Sanyo
Sanyo Basic User's Handbook
Sanyo MBC™ 550/555 User's Handbook
Sanyo MBC™ Business Software in Basic
Sanyo MBC™ 775 User's Handbook

Software
pfs User's Handbook (Summer 85)
Appleworks User's Handbook (Summer 85)
TK! Solver User's Handbook

Operating Systems
DOS 3.0 User's Handbook (Fall 85)
OASIS User's Handbook (Summer 85)
PICK® User's Handbook (Fall 85)
XENIX™ User's Handbook
CP/M Simplified

Programs and Models
SuperCalc³ Models
Lotus 1-2-3 Models
Multiplan Models
Apple Macintosh® Business Software in Basic
Kaypro® Business Software in Basic
IBM PC® Business Software in Basic
Sanyo MBC® Business Software in Basic

Atari
Atari XE User's Handbook
Atari ST User's Handbook
Atari ST Business Software in Basic
The Atari XL Program Book (Summer 85)
Atari XL™ User's Handbook
User's Handbook to the Atari 400/800

Lotus
Lotus 1-2-3 Advanced User's Guide (Fall 85)
Lotus 1-2-3 Models
Symphony Command Language Programmer's Guide

Tandy
The Model 100 Program Book
Inside the TRS-80 Model 100
Basic Business Package for TRS-80® Computers

Miscellaneous
65C02 Programmer's Guide (Fall 85)
Speech Systems for Your Microcomputer
Programs for Electronic Circuit Design
Okidata® Printer User's Handbook
CBASIC Simplified